SHANE CONNOLLY'S
wedding
FLOWERS

Photography by Jan Baldwin

T

Trafalgar Square Publishing

For the friends who made 14.12.91 such an unforgettable day, florally and musically—and especially my bride C.C.K.C.

First published in the United States of America in 1998 by Trafalgar Square Publishing, North Pomfret, Vermont 05053

First paperback edition 2003

Printed and bound in Hong Kong
Printed and bound in China

Editorial Director Suzannah Gough
Managing Editor Kate Bell
Copy Editor Sarah Sears
Editorial Assistance Tanya Robinson, Jane Royston

Commissioning Art Editor Leslie Harrington
Designer Amanda Lerwill
Stylist Sylvie Jones
Assistant Stylist Portland Mitchell
Hair and Makeup Evelynne Stoikou,
   Barbara Braunlich, Firyal Arneil

Production Suzanne Sharpless
Index Hilary Bird

The publisher would like to thank Rupert Crew for permission to reproduce an extract from *The Glass of Fashion* by Cecil Beaton, and The Society of Authors on behalf of the Bernard Shaw Estate for permission to reproduce an extract from *Pygmalion*.

ISBN 1-57076-247-3
Library of Congress Control Number: 2003100436

Contents

Setting a style

Weddings are rather like theatrical productions, with variations only in the pieces being performed; some resemble alternative fringe comedy while others compete with full-scale grand opera for drama and histrionics.

Unlike most stage productions, however, the whole show is usually produced, designed, stage-managed, and directed by a few of the stars, none of whom generally has had much—if any—previous experience, either as a performer or in any of the backstage roles. As the date of the performance approaches, all the disparate components vie for attention. Each option is mooted and discussed; decisions are reached and, gradually, the initial aims and directions are modified and compromises are made. Only on the day itself do all these various elements settle together when—perhaps colored by exhaustion, temptation, or budgetary restraint—they often give a rather muddled performance.

I find that this is particularly true of the esthetic aspects of the day. Although these should never predominate or obscure the significance of a wedding, an ill-considered decorative scheme or visual jungle is often very distracting. The antithesis—an imaginative, attractive, holistic theme—lends dignity even to the smallest wedding. Of course, it is much easier to describe such a unified decorative scheme than to achieve it. Sometimes a professional party-planner is employed to find a theme, and to use his or her experience and specialist contacts to implement it. This approach avoids "too many cooks spoiling the broth," but it can mean that one's personal instinct becomes lost in compromise.

Each of the twenty weddings in this book has a different "feeling"—theme is perhaps too strong a word. Each was inspired by a dress or location, or by a combination of the two, and each uses flowers to clarify this "feeling," arranged in such a way that they create a distinctive ambience and build a visual link between the bridal party and the setting. They illustrate just how individual inspiration actually is, and how different one can dare to be.

Weddings should never be a mere visual remix of one's past experiences as a guest. Nor are there rules that guarantee success, although it is perhaps worth noting that, if there are to be various contributors, the best results tend to be produced when everyone knows what everyone else is doing: the hairdresser's proposed hairstyle or the caterer's final choice of tablecloth color will both influence the florist's flowers, and it is this latter who alone can link everything—whatever the bride's desired look. Actually designing the decorations and choosing the flowers can begin only once this scheme has been established.

I find that, even today, the majority of first-time brides prefer to look more feminine than daring—though second-time brides are usually the opposite! For some, this femininity is rooted in a traditional image of the bride—albeit one invented comparatively recently—with

OPPOSITE *Stating the obvious perhaps, yet this Grecian-inspired wedding dress is both enhanced and made complete with the addition of the classical leafy victor's garland. The bouquet is less stylized but again echoes the lines of the dress in its fluid, sweeping elegance.*

ABOVE *Flowers are infinitely adaptable and should suit the wearer and her personality rather than merely conforming to traditional bridal expectations. Used like this, to trim a jaunty hat, they become part of a fashionable accessory and match this bride's chosen image in a unique way.*

a wedding dress characterized by some sort of historical element or inspiration. Interestingly, unlike their mainstream colleagues, most bridal designers seem unaware of the dichotomy between historical fashion and contemporary requirements, and blithely borrow and combine ingredients from different epochs, ignoring the fact that historical costumes can look incongruous in today's world. Flowers can help to blend these disparate elements to create a harmonious result.

I find that the bride's choice of dress is one of the best starting-points as it says so much about her taste and her vision of the wedding. I try to use flowers that will not clash with the style and period of the dress. In this respect, I find contemporary paintings a rich source, both for colors and for styles of decoration.

There are no rules to say that flowers have to be carried as a posy or bouquet—this book shows several equally beautiful options which are designed to enhance details and trimmings on dresses, rather than hiding them. When placed in the bride's hair, flowers should be used to raise a contemporary hairstyle to a level of elegance or scale appropriate to the dress. However, there is no need to use flowers to achieve this—look at *all* the alternatives. Whatever is chosen, it will look best if it is there for a purpose—holding hair in place, for example, rather than merely balancing on top of an elaborate coiffure. Flowers for bridesmaids and attendants generally look better if they are less sophisticated than those of the bride, while remaining complementary in style. This can be achieved by using humbler flowers, or by contrasting a mixture of blooms with all one type for the bride.

ABOVE *Gloriously simple: this "daisy-chain" headdress is sweet and uncontrived. It makes the perfect choice for a very young bridesmaid as it is light enough to sit happily on fine undressed hair without any uncomfortable hairclips or combs.*

Not everyone has access to the ideal settings that we found for this book, but flowers can certainly help to tie the elements together to create a unique, appropriate atmosphere or ambience. With their help it is perfectly possible to build up complete illusions in a marquee, for example, or to create wonderfully apposite and distracting table arrangements.

Larger decorations, in particular, need a firm starting-point if they are to provide ongoing links between the many aspects of the day. Getting the scale right is vital. Imagine the space filled with people and consider the degree of available light before deciding on the decorations. Scale in this context is not just about physical size, but about scale of color, too; mixed colors look very different when viewed at a distance than when seen at close range.

Finally, a word on behalf of the flowers themselves. So often, in the unnatural contortions of contemporary flower-arranging, the delicacy of a bloom is lost or the stems so densely packed that the wood of beauty is lost for the trees of plenty. I abhor the use of flowers simply because of a perceived "need" to have them, and I believe that the loveliness of individual flowers should be the *raison d'être* of a particular style of arrangement. I also want to put in a word for the more unusual "modest" flowers such as primroses, violets, and forget-me-nots, so often ignored in favor of some fancy, exotic bloom, palid in its out-of-season colors and rather tired after a long flight. Many more truly memorable schemes would be created if florists were a little more imaginative, and their clients a little more trusting and flexible.

BELOW *The decoration of large spaces is always more successful if a unifying scheme is agreed before individual elements are designed. This not only results in greater visual impact, but makes the design process simpler, as guidelines and criteria are firmly established.*

classic

SOME BRIDES FIND the label "classic" offputting in relation to weddings, as they take the word to suggest a severity that some think unromantic, or to denote a strong adherence to tradition, which might also imply "old-fashioned." Neither, of course, is true, and this wedding is certainly a classic. It has refinement but also an appealing individuality; no single word can define it because, like a personality, it has many components and nuances.

As ever, the cut and look of the dress supplied my initial inspiration. I felt that it had some of the qualities of the so-called "New Look" of the late 1940s and '50s, initially the brainchild of Christian Dior, whose designs, it was once said, gave women the feeling of being "charmingly costumed," though his tailored lines were anything but frothy. This dress possesses something of that faintly romantic charm, with its sweet organza sleeves —its only concession to decoration—and trailing skirts.

I felt that the deliciously scented lily-of-the-valley would be the perfect flower for the dress, because it, too, has a delightful old-fashioned quality which is light and undemanding while being simple and elegant—especially when used alone. In my method, I was inspired by the wonderful eighteenth-century rococo plasterwork in the reception rooms, where plaster flowers scoop and drape,

LEFT The short sleeves of the bride's dress are trimmed with dainty garlands of lily-of-the-valley, and replace the more traditional hand-held bouquet. A similar garland anchors her tulle veil.
OPPOSITE A towering green-and-white arrangement of flowers and foliage balances the frothy ambience of this intricate plasterwork.

A Gentle Classic

A distinctly subtle interpretation of classically inspired themes gives these wedding flowers an ethereal quality of lightness and refinement. This is definitely chic without severity, an effect achieved through the essentially modest and simple qualities of the flowers chosen.

"... Dior is the Watteau of dressmaking—full of nuances, chic, delicate, and timely ..."

Cecil Beaton

garlanding door-frames and plaster busts in an utterly charming and frivolous way. To copy the opulent mixed flowers of the plaster garlands would have weighed down the dress both physically and visually, whereas these lilies-of-the-valley have the reverse effect, softening the look of the dress to suit the ethereal surroundings—the difference between inspiration and plagiarism. Without spoiling the sleek and contemporary late twentieth-century design, they give a hint of the eighteenth century. Moreover, the circlets emphasize the prettiness of the short sleeves; whereas a bouquet would inevitably have drawn the spectator's eye down to the hands.

The bridal veil was anchored by another matching wreath around an elegant small chignon—not a style that would suit everyone. A tiara headdress of lilies-of-the-valley, or a more elaborate skullcap with the delicate stems wired so as to clasp the head gently might be more flattering for a bride with shorter hair. I used the same flowers for the bridegroom's buttonhole too, in a welcome variation from the ubiquitous rosebud or carnation.

Lilies-of-the-valley had by now almost become the *leitmotif* of the wedding. However, the shortness of their stems is slightly limiting, so when it came to designing the flowers for the ceremony and reception I decided to use them only for the table decorations, where height was not a problem and where their delicacy and scent could be fully enjoyed. Just to be a little different, I combined them with lime-green, dark-green and softly variegated helxine plants. These were arranged in strips in a rectangular silver tray on the main long table—a faint echo of the formal green parterres which would have been in vogue when the rooms were decorated. Small posies of lily-of-the-valley surrounded by more helxines decorated each place setting.

OPPOSITE The bride's modest headdress and sleeve trim were created by binding small wired clusters of lilies-of-the-valley on to a premeasured length of fine wire—both for flexibility and to make them light and comfortable to wear. Several strands of cotton thread were sewn in place before the dress was put on, and the garlands tied on to the sleeves at the last minute. The bridegroom's buttonhole continues this delicate theme.

RIGHT A medley of green helxine plants, arranged quaintly in stripes in a rectangular silver tray, makes an unusual centerpiece for the main luncheon table, while between each guest's place-setting complementary posies of lilies-of-the-valley—the theme flower of the whole wedding—stand in small hexagonal silver bowls surrounded by more helxines. Circular tables for other guests could also be decorated with larger versions of these little posies.

ABOVE The solid architecture of the church creates a very different mood to the ornate and capricious plasterwork of the eighteenth-century reception rooms, and the flowers I chose reflected this change. These daisies have a naive charm which complements the solid medieval-style building. They are arranged to outline the stark angularity while hinting at the frothiness of the reception rooms. A large mixed arrangement of sorbus (*S. aria* 'Lutescens' and *S. cashmiriana*), broom, Canterbury bells, marguerites, guelder roses (*Viburnum opulus*), cardoon leaves (*Cynara cardunculus*), and spiraea fills a curving archway with dignified opulence.

It was not easy to design a large arrangement to decorate the elaborate staircase—one that would sit happily both with the intricate plasterwork and with the delicate bridal flowers. I chose to use equally delicate spring blossoms and arranged them to look like huge fountains so that, while retaining the melting softness and gentle elegance of the whole scheme, the result was tall and dramatic. To do this, I fixed blocks of wet florist's foam around a pole for height, securing this in a floridly ornate urn for stability and solidity.

The church had a completely different look and ambience to the reception venue. The architecture and decoration—correctly termed "French Gothic"—were more heavy and solid, although their lines still had a certain fluidity. To reproduce the frothy flower arrangement that I had created for the staircase seemed somehow frivolous in such a serious setting, and yet a link was needed. For this reason, I decided to use the same flowers, but in large tumbling arrangements placed in arched niches around the church. Then, using the borders of some medieval tapestries as a touchstone, I encircled the middle of the church with a continuous garland of marguerites. Lilies-of-the-valley would have been sublime here, but prohibitively expensive, and the daisies were an obvious substitute, being equally charming and lacking in artifice. Again, the use of a single type of flower makes a strong statement and balances the frothy tendencies of the large arrangements.

The bridesmaid's flowers were chosen to echo the daisies in the church. It seemed entirely appropriate that her flowers should be linked more to the church than to the reception, given that her primary role—as attendant to the bride during the marriage ceremony—placed her in this context. Mirroring the bride's flowers, I made a simple daisy-chain headdress for the bridesmaid, which was as fine and delicate as that of the bride but with an unsophisticated innocence that is perfect for a tiny person. A bunch of artlessly gathered marguerites gave the ideal finishing touch—these look charming and simple, however they are held.

TOP LEFT A delicate alabaster urn on a small occasional table holds an arrangement of flowers and foliage which links elements of the whole flower scheme. It includes marguerites, euphorbia (*E. nicaeensis*), spiraea, rosemary, catmint, and broom.

ABOVE AND LEFT Choosing to echo the daisies I used in the church for this young bridesmaid was an easy and effective decision. Her "daisy-chain" headdress mirrors the bride's circlets of lilies-of-the-valley, and is just as refreshingly unaffected. Rather than attempting to match the bride's sophisticated sleeve detail on such a young child, it was simpler and more appropriate to give her a matching bunch of daisies to carry. These are purposely left "unarranged," and as natural-looking as possible, in order to create the sort of scene-stealing picture of total innocence of which the most treasured wedding memories are made.

ABOVE A beautiful combination of elegance and femininity. The elaborate lace of this dress might so easily have been a difficult background for flowers but the combination of the waxy perfection of stephanotis with the glossy green of camellia leaves is both sophisticated enough to give a sense of dignity amid the frills, and dainty enough not to overpower the delicate patterns of the lace.

A subtle mixture

of apparently disparate elements—romance, sophistication, couture chic, and touching piety—creates this picture of timeless bridal elegance.

Generally speaking, most florists would not choose layers of billowing lace as a background for a floral bouquet. it is too easy to lose shape and definition amidst the folds of this most delicately elaborate of fabrics. Sometimes they are tempted to match the background with an equally frothy bouquet—a bundle of gypsophila perhaps—and produce a meringue effect, spoiling the essentially classical lightness of this style of gown.

The secret, I think, is to use small flowers but in a clean, sophisticated way. Stephanotis is a traditional ingredient of wedding bouquets but it is generally mixed with other elements and used mainly to supply scent. Its waxy whiteness, however, is exquisite in its own right and it makes a deliciously elegant bouquet—especially when combined with dark green foliage.

Carrying flowers on a prayerbook is an old-fashioned idea yet in keeping with the traditional style of this dress, and the prayerbook serves to separate the lace from the flowers; it is like a frame for a floral picture. The size of the book restricts the size of the bouquet too—appropriate for a dress like this, which needs little embellishment.

Further flounces of lace in a veil would not flatter such a frothy dress, but this elaborate, sleek hairstyle has enough volume to balance the visual weight of the huge skirts. More wired stephanotis flowers, resembling jeweled hairpins, were placed in a regular pattern through the bride's hair to create a fresh interpretation of a very traditional look.

RIGHT Each stephanotis flower was individually wired before this small trailing posy was assembled. It was then attached to an antique prayerbook, which makes a wonderfully effective frame for this jewel-like little bouquet.

BELOW The bride's elaborately coiled hairstyle was dotted with single stephanotis flowers. I was inspired both by the polka-dot pattern in the lace of her dress and by a portrait of Austria's last Empress, in which her hair was sprinkled with diamond stars.

THE DRESS CHOSEN by this bride reflects a strong and refined sense of judgement. The epitome of elegance—restrained, understated, appropriate—it illustrates the perfect subtlety of chic, and is completely at home in this sumptuous hotel where its simplicity shines like a beacon.

Although it might be tempting to make a wonderfully clever or colorful bouquet that stands out against a plain background like this, the last thing a florist should do is to spoil this simplicity with flowers that detract from, rather than add to, the overall look. I was inspired, instead, to emphasize one fashion detail—the sweeping train falling asymmetrically from one shoulder. I had seen bouquets that resembled large cabbage-roses, or "malmaisons" as they are sometimes called, made by wiring pleated clusters of rose petals together. The tailored look of the dress also reminded me of the work of the famous Coco Chanel, whose trademark was a large silk camellia worn on a severe suit. The two thoughts combined to inspire my flowers here.

I decided to use fresh creamy white tulip petals because their large size and sensuous texture seemed even more suited than roses to this dress. Two or three petals were pleated and threaded together with fine silver wire, then carefully bound around a single intact tulip, its own

LEFT These chic and contemporary wedding flowers use the classic combination of fresh white and rich green; the bride's are worn on one shoulder, and the bridesmaid's carried in an unusual tied posy.
OPPOSITE Decorating a low table, a mound of white-and-green double tulips and lime-green euphorbia (*E. cyparissias*) in a glass bowl.

City Chic

The flowers for this city wedding act as the perfect accessory—they are confidently understated and apposite, intrinsically beautiful, and completely devoid of any extraneous detail ... a feast for the discerning eye.

LEFT An antique carved wooden fireplace is given a simple modern treatment. A huge glass bowl is packed with white double tulips and long-stemmed French tulips, some *Ornithogalum arabicum*, lime clusters of guelder rose (*Viburnum opulus*) and euphorbias (*E. characias* subsp. *wulfenii* and *E. cyparissias.*) It makes a refreshing and stylish alternative to a more traditional trailing mantelshelf arrangement and by deliberately avoiding any imitation of it, succeeds in drawing attention to the decorative carved fruits at each side of the mirror.

petals gently flexed back to hide the wires, until one large flower was created. This type of floral creation is really a job for the expert, but if you want to try it, choose petals from tulips that have been cut for several days. If they are too fresh they will split as you wire them. Surprisingly, "malmaisons" last well, although I added a collar of stiff camellia leaves here, both for visual effect and to support any petals that might wilt as the day progressed.

I came up with this bunch of ranunculus for the bridesmaid, who deserved equally stylish flowers. Solid white, framed by dark green, it reflects the bride's flowers but is less sophisticated.

Finally I had to decorate the venue. Its Edwardian grandeur might, for a different wedding, have inspired genteel arrangements in soft pastels, but this bride was determined that she wanted to make a big contemporary statement. I therefore decided to use classic flowers to make arrangements on a scale that would suit the huge rooms—but using chunky, modern glass containers. This is a wonderfully liberating style of arranging because it encourages one to make big piles of a single flower type and, without the control of wire and florist's foam, to put together informal, asymmetrical mixtures that perfectly complement this whole look.

LEFT The bridesmaid's unusual and stylish posy of closely packed white ranunculus. The stems have been left quite long and covered with a few aspidistra leaves tied with braided grass.

BELOW LEFT A contemporary mixed group in a massive glass vase: a sprawling asymmetrical mixture of tulips, *Euphorbia wulfenii*, and huge branches of copper beech (*Fagus purpurea*), *Viburnum lantana* and tuberose (*Polianthes tuberosa*) form an angular shape which perfectly matches the sculptural glass-topped console table.

BELOW A closer look at the bride's flowers—a real conversation piece! Individual tulip petals were pleated, wired, and reassembled around a single tulip to give this fantastical silken camellia appearance, the edging of immaculate green camellia leaves fueling the illusion.

Severe yet feminine:

the tailored suit, once the only option for the city bride married by a judge, is now a most stylish alternative. This trim of exquisitely romantic flowers provides the ultimate finishing touch.

A smart city suit was once the only real alternative to a white wedding dress for brides. Perhaps it was thought to convey a more appropriate degree of formality and seriousness than might a beautiful, but not bridal, dress. Whatever the reason, the results were often severe.

Although equally dignified suits are being made today, they now tend to be characterized by a softness that comes from gentler colors or less rigid fabrics. This version is a deliciously vague shade of blue-gray with a gray satin collar and matching dainty purse.

It was the frivolous hat, however, combining the two colors, which was the starting point for the wedding's floral scheme. Inspired by my successful creations with tulips (see pages 20–23,) I decided to make rose-petal "blooms" out of the pale lemon rose 'Hollywood' to trim this hat. A pastel color was the obvious choice, and somehow lemon is fresher than pinks or peaches.

I created two "flowers," each around a rose center, rather than an intact rose-flower. The first was more full-blown than the tulip version, the second was smaller, to decorate the bride's satin purse. Both were edged with their own leaves and left under damp tissue paper until the last minute.

The tables were decorated with posies of intact roses of the same variety, in tall silver sundae glasses. A sprinkling of rose-petal confetti gave the final romantic touch.

ABOVE The bride wears a simple dove-gray suit, its tailored lines softened with some rather special pale lemon roses. Like the previous bride's "camellias," they are, in fact, individually wired rose petals reassembled to form a voluptuous cabbage-rose shape—officially called a "malmaison" by florists.

OPPOSITE On the table a posy of the same rose (*Rosa* 'Hollywood'), left as nature intended. It sits on an antique mirror glass which reflects the elaborate ceiling and gives a soft floating effect.

OVERLEAF LEFT The bride is showered with fresh rose-petal confetti.
OVERLEAF RIGHT (clockwise from top left) *Rosa* 'Hollywood' a pale lemon variety; voluptuous roses are used to decorate the rim of the bride's two-toned straw hat—even the bud is "hand-made" to ensure that it is the right size and shape; aluminum baskets are filled with rose-petal confetti for the guests to use as the happy couple depart; a suitably dainty bloom is used to decorate the bride's tiny purse.

THE ANCIENT CIVILIZATIONS of Greece and Rome have been plundered for inspiration at regular intervals throughout the centuries. This process has injected a fresh and distinctive elegance into all types of design, coming as it frequently does after periods of devotion to more romantic influences. In the wake of the "frothy" wedding styles of the 1980s and the correspondingly overblown flowers that went with them, the restraint of classically inspired themes has re-emerged in recent years.

This dress is a perfect example. It is timelessly elegant and stylishly unelaborate and yet it is, in essence, a traditional wedding dress. Such a clever and beautiful reinterpretation of existing elements is, to me, the essence of true innovation. Accordingly, my flowers have to abide by the same principles.

With this in mind, I decided to create a large, flowing style of bridal bouquet, both because it would flatter the long, slim lines of the dress and because it is the most traditional shape for a bride to choose and therefore a real challenge as regards fresh interpretation. These designs are usually wired so that the flowers can be bent to "flow" at the required angle, but I decided to use flowers with natural movement and simply to tie them together. Cutting stephanotis trails from bought plants seemed

LEFT Trails of stephanotis are supported and separated by stems of large-leaved ruscus (*R. hypoglossum*) in the bride's long, tied bouquet.
OPPOSITE A cast-iron urn is filled with cascades of bride's blossom (*Philadelphus* 'Belle Etoile') and *Rosa* 'Rambling Rector', plumes of aruncus (*A. dioicus*), clumps of golden iris, and campanula.

Pure Grecian

The pure classicism of ancient Rome and Greece is the inspiration behind a wedding scheme that is both highly individual and uncompromisingly elegant. It provides an appealingly fresh interpretation of the traditional all-white wedding theme.

the ideal answer, but these do tend to appear "limp" because of their heavy character. I therefore used a few stems of stiffly branched foliage as the basis of the bouquet, trailing the stephanotis around and through it—allowing it to flow rather than simply hang. The cut ends were wrapped in damp absorbent cotton and plastic to keep the flowers fresh, then wrapped in white silk ribbon to hide them.

Following the obviously classical inspiration of the dress and this setting, I based the headdresses on styles that often feature in ancient Greek and Roman frescoes. For the bride, the leaves were attached with fine wire in a regular overlapping pattern to a high curving wire frame which, in turn, was attached to another wire to encircle the head and fasten invisibly under the roll of hair. This headdress could have been left as plain green leaves or might be made entirely of gilded or silver leaves. However, I was surrounded here by so much greenery that I felt a few white flowers would add definition and create a stronger link with the bouquet.

As the bridesmaid's dress was simply a shorter version of the wedding dress, I believed that her flowers should resemble those of the bride quite closely—while not, of course, detracting from the latter's starring role. I started with a more modest headdress, which simply decorated the sides of the head without rising like a regal tiara at the front. I made her a long bouquet, too, but one designed to be carried as a plain bunch of flowers—less easy than it appears, for such studied artlessness usually requires some practice if the bouquet is not to look stiff.

I decided to let the classical architecture of the setting speak for itself. I resisted the temptation to decorate doorways and garlanded pillars; instead, I rented classical urns to stand on the tables and filled them to dramatic effect with armfuls of white and cream flowers. Massive fiberglass urns can be rented to provide the feeling of classical architecture in a less appropriate setting. In the fall, for a rich, cornucopean look, trailing vines and heaps of grapes in large stone-effect urns could be echoed on the tables by marble platters of grapes and leaves.

ABOVE The bridesmaid's bouquet is a sheaf of philadelphus, with stems of dainty white campanula (*C. persicifolia*), echoing the starry shape of the stephanotis both in the bride's bouquet and in the bridesmaid's simple garland headdress. This style of bouquet is more suitable for a confident adult bridesmaid than a child, not only because of its scale but because, unless it is carried elegantly, it can look graceless and rather unbecoming.

TOP LEFT Several stephanotis plants were unraveled slowly and painstakingly from the training wires on which they had been growing and generously entwined around the wedding cake, the pots hidden under the silver cake-stand.

ABOVE The bridesmaid's simple flowers are designed to seem very much part of her whole hair treatment; they emerge from, but appear securely anchored in, a loose chignon.

LEFT The bride's similar headdress is a high garland tiara of camellia leaves, their proportions and shiny richness being more appropriate here than the traditional victor's laurel leaves. Buds and flowers of stephanotis are added at the sides in a regular pattern.

FLOWERS FOR SUMMER weddings can easily become over-exuberant. Plentiful and relatively inexpensive supplies of most varieties make restraint a challenge to both bride and florist. Sometimes I find this abundance excessive, especially if the context is classical and refined.

The bridal gown here is perfect for its setting, combining historical and traditional elements—heavy duchess satin and sweeping skirts—with a plainness that is contemporary as well. Once again, the temptation is to use this plainness as a background for a state-of-the-art floral extravaganza, but restraint—the basis of all elegance—is more important in this case.

The bride was already "decorated," her elaborate upswept hairstyle surmounted by a substantial glittering tiara. I felt that the flowers should not compete and so chose to make a simple bouquet of gardenias, flowers with an impeccable air of elegance and unmatchable scent, and a perfect partner for this grand, aristocratic image. Each flower must be wired with extreme care as they bruise very easily; they are cushioned in the bouquet with sprigs of their own glossy leaves and a few stephanotis flowers.

I thought that a veil would spoil the elaborate hair treatment and high tiara, and instead outlined the curve of the hair by nestling several gardenia flowers in it.

LEFT A bride in the grand tradition carries a bouquet of gardenias.
OPPOSITE Occasional tables are decorated with small stone urns filled with cones of sliced limes, scented stephanotis, clumps of lime-green helxine, and rich green camellia leaves, to give height while leaving as much space as possible on these restricted surfaces.

A Classical Tradition

Elegance, scent, and a certain lightness of touch characterize the flowers for this traditionally grand wedding with a definite contemporary twist. Ostentation is shunned; the focus instead is a simple and limited palette of components and exquisite attention to detail.

"... she imagined herself acting the new part of a fine lady; and so got on pretty well, though the tight dress gave her a side-ache, [and] the train kept getting under her feet ..."

Louisa M. Alcott *Little Women*

ABOVE A sweep of creamy white gardenias, matching the pearls in the bridal tiara, demonstrates that flowers in the hair *can* look completely sophisticated. Each flower is wired, set individually into the finished chignon and held in place by its own wires.
RIGHT An elegant wired bouquet of deliciously scented gardenias. They are arranged with their own foliage and a few stephanotis flowers to bring the scent factor into an even higher realm.

Again these were individually wired, with the wire acting as a hairclip holding each flower in place. If using gardenias without leaves to cushion them, as I have done here, it is a good idea to add small loops of green-taped wire beneath each of the lower flower petals, or a cuff of stiff paper to hold them in place, because gardenias are inclined to point downward as they dehydrate.

The bridesmaid's headdress was designed to echo the bride's hair decoration, but was simpler and less sophisticated, and again only one type of flower was used for both headdress and posy. For the headdress, individually wired delphinium blooms were re-mounted to look like a growing delphinium flower spike. Made in a graceful tapered curve, it was securely fastened by being attached to a fine braided rope of hair that firmly outlined the nape of the bridesmaid's neck. A small posy of wired delphinium flowers and the leftover tips and side-shoots made a simple spray for her to hold.

Decorations for the tables could easily have been bowls of growing gardenias but, with a stand-up reception, the tables are generally quite modest in size and few in number, making it possible to do something more interesting. The guests must be able to use the limited surface area, so small-based urns are invaluable. Their height is also useful in a tall room. I made the elegant topiary decorations on bases of pre-shaped florist's foam, covered in chicken wire for extra strength. Their architectural style seemed to suit the classical room. The shape was gradually built up, using sliced limes (more decorative than the whole fruit) placed as regularly as possible, stephanotis, to echo the bride's flowers, clumps of growing helxine held in place by clips of stub-wire, and a fringe of glossy camellia leaves. The whole arrangement can be covered in plastic wrap until the last moment, to keep the limes fresh.

For the ceremony, huge urns were filled with white delphiniums to match the bridesmaid's flowers, and to maintain the measure of restraint in the variety of flowers used. Urns like these would be equally at home if large-scale decorations were required in these reception rooms.

ABOVE The bridesmaid's headdress is made up of individual white and cream delphinium flowers, each wired and remounted, without greenery. Obviously unsuitable for a very young bridesmaid with fine hair, this style of headdress can be secured in long hair on a base of two fine braids. A posy of delphinium flowers and tips completes the picture.

COFFEE AND CREAM might, at first, seem an unusual color combination to choose for weddings. Certainly, on some brides, it could look dowdy and unexciting but, given the right bride and the right setting, it can strike a note of perfect elegance, worthy of the altogether more stylish appellation "café au lait."

These beautiful creamy rooms, with their worn stone floors, have an easy and subtle refinement, and no distracting details. In the soft fall light, with its bounty of fading foliage, the rooms were the inspiration behind and perfect foil for this dress of dusky coffee-colored damask and ivory satin.

My favorite bridal flowers are those that complete the picture, rather than making an individual statement. Those chosen here—understated both in style and color—do exactly that.

I made a very simple headdress for the bride by inserting three wired ivory-colored roses under the comb of her veil. This suited her short hairstyle and worked well with the scale of the bouquet, a dainty combination of creamy flowers and bronzed foliage in a light but compact posy. As all of the flowers were wired there were no clumsy stems and the slim handle of the bouquet could be bound in cream silk. Moreover, being

LEFT Simple and chic: the flowers for the bride and bridesmaid in shades of cream and buff with chocolate-brown foliage.
OPPOSITE The tables are decorated with square boxes covered in preserved magnolia leaves and filled with snowberry, bouvardia, and white heather, brightened by trumpeting stems of eucharis.

Café au Lait

The flowers for this fall wedding are distinguished by their classically understated elegance. The usual exuberance of the season is handled with restraint—using a softly faded color scheme of buff stone, creamy ivory and warm browns.

small, it neither obscures nor incorporates the bow on the front of the dress; the trimmings must always be given careful consideration when designing the accompanying flowers.

The bridesmaid, in matching fabrics, carries a small bouquet which again blends perfectly with the colors of both dresses. It is difficult to design similarly subtle headdresses for young girls. Delicate designs that need to stay attached for any length of time, often require elaborate hairstyles which can look precocious. The usual compromise is a circlet of flowers.

The design shown here is one solution. The plain fabric-covered Alice band stays firmly in place and the delicate sprays at either side are not overly florid.

To decorate the room, I rented old stone garden urns which seemed at home in the architectural style of the venue, and filled them with armfuls of fall foliage interspersed with a few garden flowers. For the tables, I made elegant containers from wooden boxes covered with glycerine-painted magnolia leaves, then filled them with a mound of heather, bouvardia, snowberries, and stems of eucharis.

OPPOSITE A stone urn filled with a glorious medley of fall foliage and "garden cuttings," including oak, field maple, forsythia, stephanandra, montbretia, amaranthus, *Hydrangea paniculata*, sunflowers, and an unknown old rose—all in rich shades of cream, buff, brown, bronze, and green. At this time of year such an arrangement is an economical pleasure—to add cultivated flowers would seem almost vulgar.

ABOVE The understated bridal bouquet is smaller and neater than usual. A few stems of roses (*Rosa* 'Iceberg' and

R. 'Ivory') nestle quietly amid creamy snowberries, scented tuberoses, and brown foliage.

TOP RIGHT For the bridesmaid's headdress I bought an Alice band and bound it in fabric to match the dress. Small, wired clusters of snowberry, heather, and foliage have then been sewn firmly in place at each side.

RIGHT The bridesmaid's tied posy is made of similar ingredients, to blend subtly with the gentle colors of her dress. The result is a unified picture rather than a statement.

Elegant yet romantic:

the same combination of subtle colors is treated more theatrically here, as the restrained scheme of the previous pages is replaced with the exuberance of an eighteenth-century sepia costume print.

Fall's subtle tints need not always be treated with modesty; they can be just as effective as part of a more exuberant, romantic scheme.

Inspired by a brocade dress worn with a satin-lined opera cape, I combined tuberose, bouvardia, heather, and brown leaves to make a classical victor's wreath for the bride's hair—an excellent way of creating the illusion of a long style worn up. Her short hair was simply twisted at a few points to give a secure base upon which to "clip" the necessarily light flowers. The overall effect is more in keeping with the period feel of the ensemble than short hair would be, yet the bride looks natural and avoids uncomfortable hairpieces.

The bouquet is a piece of frivolity—a fan of flowers trimmed with a coffee-colored silk tassel. It consists of wired clusters and stems arranged into a flat-backed fan shape, with an added backing of preserved magnolia leaves to give a cleaner outline.

Decorations for the reception needed to be equally romantic and generous, and I decided that garlands of rich, bronze oak leaves caught up with clusters of ivory berries and silk ribbons—echoing the crescent in the bride's hair—would be perfect. In a classical setting, these garlands should be fixed to drape in a regular rhythm; in less grand surroundings looser, more informal swags might be more appropriate.

OPPOSITE AND ABOVE The same color scheme with a new, dramatically romantic interpretation. The bride wears a classical crescent headdress, with a central loop and trails of silk ribbon to break the line and draw attention to the sensual nape of her neck. Meanwhile her unique and rather stylized bouquet in the shape of a fan was inspired by the unusual flowing opera cape of cream-lined coffee brocade. The success of such a stylized bouquet lies in the way that it is held. It must appear to be a fan and not a bouquet. For a more floral effect, lilies-of-the-valley would look like delicate old lace against dark magnolia leaves, and would also lend a sweet charm to the headdress.

BRIDAL FASHIONS frequently look to the past for inspiration and this dress is a perfect example of how effective composite styles can be. Its simple lines are almost medieval and yet the sophisticated tailoring is reminiscent of Art Deco's faintly austere fashions, with no frivolous details. The bride's flowers should, I felt, exude the same simplicity, sophistication, and elegance.

The calla, or arum, lily is a perfect starting point. Its clean, sculptural lines are stylistically right for the period, while its velvety, almost fleshy, texture is sensuous and sophisticated rather than traditionally sweet and pretty. I designed a very dramatic bouquet which is daringly different in the way that it trails on to the floor in a slender column of green and white. The bouquet was inspired by the flamboyant, massive jewelry typical of the late 1920s and '30s, which was often worn with simple dresses. Bear in mind on which side it is to be carried before it is made. The outline was created with wired trails of clean, green ivy and then the wired calla flowers were added singly—more densely at the top than at the bottom, where smaller blooms were attached directly to the ivy trails. The resulting "handle" of wires, which would be visible from some angles, was bound with toning silk ribbon.

LEFT A pedestal arrangement contains arching branches of camellia foliage, eucalyptus, and lichen-covered larch twigs, with sprays of calla lilies, euphorbia (*E. fulgens*) and long-stemmed creamy "French" tulips.
OPPOSITE A graceful sweep of waxy calla lilies and ivy for the bridal bouquet, with delicate jasmine trimming the cloche-style veil.

Art Deco

The sleek sculptural feel of the Art Deco era is evoked in the decorations for this sophisticated winter wedding. Sculptured calla lilies and satiny tulips are combined with icy gray foliage, glossy green camellia leaves and ivy for classical effect.

Using similar flowers and proportions for the hair would overpower the tailored cloche-style veil, so I chose instead to make a small, trim garland of jasmine. Sprays were cut from a growing plant and bound straight on to a short piece of wire with florist's tape. This was bent to a graceful curve—to follow the shape of the bride's head and to echo the sweeping bouquet—and then attached over the sheer fabric. It perfectly complements the *soigné* and elegant combination of short hair and tightly fitted veil.

Again, when it came to the setting, the key word was sophistication. The decorations needed to be grand in scale, and architectural in design, to look as if they belonged. It is a good idea to imagine the room full of standing people to ascertain which features might still be visible. Quite often, high mantelshelves are ideal: being part of the room, the effect is strong and architectural

rather than superimposed and merely decorative. Here I used a long metal trough filled with wet florist's foam and chicken wire, a good heavy base for a sprawling style of arrangement. Heavy branches were placed at the sides and back, physically and visually to balance the weight of heavy flowers trailing at the front.

If existing architectural features are minimal, another possibility in a large room is an arrangement on a pedestal or column. I tend to rent pieces like the fiberglass stand I used here because then I can choose something in keeping with the setting or the look I am trying to create.

Finally: the important choice of color. As a foil for the cream and white flowers, I opted for cool gray foliage—to reflect the gray walls and the winter season—together with the polished green of camellia foliage. This classic combination is the epitome of elegance.

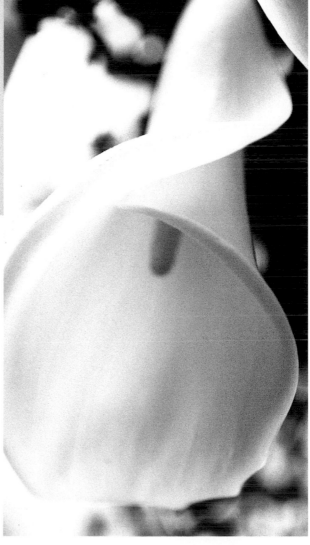

OPPOSITE A high mantelshelf is laden with a generous mound of calla lilies and tulips, that are clumped together with trailing jasmine, gray eucalyptus, and glossy, green camellia foliage. All of this will remain clearly visible above the heads of the guests.

LEFT Sprays of sweet-smelling jasmine (*Jasminum polyanthum*) are bound together into a crescent and attached to a veil at the nape of the neck to form the simplest of headdresses.

BELOW The sculptured perfection of a single calla lily.

'Harriet looked modest for the first time in her Life in a long French lace veil.'

The Journals of Elizabeth Fremantle (c.1800)

Similar ingredients

but an altogether less stylized approach are the keynotes of this less formal floral scheme, still in the Art Deco vein.

The bridal gown is more like a contemporary cocktail dress than a period costume and so my approach to the flowers was more relaxed in style. The small posy held by the bride has a frosted, silvery look inspired by her tiara—actually a broad Art Deco diamond bracelet worn bandeau-style across her head. When the bride's hair is short, as here, and the dress is sophisticated, I often avoid floral headdresses. For her bridesmaid, however, I designed a simple headdress: an Alice band of wire, hidden by a fine silk ribbon with a clump of flowers wired into place and curling prettily over the ears at each end. A simple tied bouquet of tightly packed cyclamen flowers surrounded by a cuff of their own leaves became a simpler

ABOVE A pretty winter bridal posy of cyclamen flowers and leaves, with fragrant jasmine, swirls of the tasseled catkins of *Garrya elliptica,* and frosted eucalyptus flower pods to add interest.
RIGHT An adult bridesmaid wears a simple ribbon Alice band decorated at each ear with similar floral ingredients.
OPPOSITE Wall drops make a dramatic decoration in tall rooms and are relatively economical. Here they are arranged *in situ* on plastic-backed "cages" of wet florist's foam hung from a strong picture rail. Alternatively, you could cover a block of foam with chicken wire and back it with plastic. Cream calico hides the galvanized hanging wire. A small glass urn containing an arrangement of matching flowers decorates an occasional table.

but complementary version of the bride's flowers. Even with adult bridesmaids, I do not feel that it is necessary to have flowers as sophisticated as those of the bride.

The decoration of the room is equally dramatic in its design but much less formal than on the previous pages. These wall-drop-style decorations are well suited to rooms with high ceilings and provide height without the necessity for tall flowers and foliage. Standing on a ladder, flowers can be arranged directly into florist's foam where it is hanging. Again, as in the mantelshelf arrangement, it is important to balance the design by placing foliage against the wall as well as facing forward.

To reproduce the look for a summer wedding, you could use garden roses for the bouquets and trails of roses in the wall drop; fruits could be incorporated as well, to imitate elaborately carved wood or plasterwork.

WINTER WEDDINGS often pose a challenge to the creative floral decorator, especially those planned in the aftermath of Christmas. Interesting flowers are relatively scarce, the bright jollity of Christmas seems passé and the sweet freshness of spring has not quite arrived—even in the forced blooms of the flower markets. This wedding uses the available winter ingredients in a stylized way, creating a breath of fresh air for a cold winter's day.

The inspiration came from the wonderful classical proportions of the orangery chosen for the ceremony and wedding banquet. The stone floors and tall windows give it an airy Italianate feel. When this was combined with the starkly simple silhouette of the bridal gown and its exquisite sleeve detail, I began to imagine an early Renaissance garden, the design influenced by the era's passion for classical proportion, yet without the sophistication of later eighteenth-century formal gardens.

The most striking feature of the wedding dress is the crossover detail on the sleeves. Consequently, I created a bouquet that would be held with both hands cupped, to emphasize the sleeves rather than conceal them. It is wired to fit snugly into the hands and its fresh orange, green, and white color scheme is understated so as not to distract from the hands and sleeves.

LEFT A handful of stephanotis, glossy green leaves of ruscus, small kumquats, and solanum berries make a novel and fresh winter bouquet.
OPPOSITE A stage set for the wedding feast with *faux* hedges of cut box, growing ficus trees masquerading as orange trees—with wired oranges and flowers—and clipped kumquat trees lining the long tables.

Renaissance Style

The great rebirth of classicism imbues this winter wedding with a welcomingly unseasonal freshness and vigor. An Italianate garden room is created for the wedding celebrations with the tangy citrus theme extending to the bridal flowers.

A girdle of flowers designed to leave the hands completely free was a more unusual alternative. Made on a length of thin ribbon to be as flexible as possible, it moves with the wearer. This is most important as this type of floral decoration will only work if it appears to be part of the clothing.

A similar circular garland, bound on to wire, decorated the bride's chignon, and a smaller circlet held the hair at the nape of the neck. Again the subtlety of the ingredients allowed for this complex and elaborate hair treatment which, with more floral garlands, could easily have looked overdone. To ensure that the bride feels at ease on the day, it is worth making a trial sample with silk flowers for both the belt and other such detailed headdresses.

For the room, I first rented several mature standard ficus trees. Their leaves are very similar to those of citrus trees and, with wired-on oranges and clusters of hyacinth

ABOVE This clever alternative to the wedding bouquet is an appropriately Renaissance-style girdle of green ruscus, solanum berries, and white hyacinth flowers. It maintains the citrus theme and leaves the beautiful sleeve detail unencumbered.

RIGHT The decoration for the bride's hair not only matches the girdle but seems straight out of an old Italian painting. Some sprigs of Christmas box (*Sarcococca humilis*) are added for their sweetly scented flowers.

RIGHT A garlanded buffet table: shiny laurel (*Prunus laurocerasus*) and large oranges are held together by white silken ribbons. A central tazza piled with satsumas makes a beautiful still-life.
BELOW A complementary color scheme for the entrance with growing parterres of rosemary and white crocus.

flowers for blossom, few could tell the difference. I planted the trees in large fiberglass "terracotta" pots, washed with diluted white latex paint and rubbed with wet soil for an aged look. With the addition of turf to cover the soil, the trees looked as if they had always grown there.

Next I divided the space with "box hedges," made simply by threading branches of cut box through strong wooden trellises and trimming the result. Yew cuttings would do just as well. Such hedges will last a few weeks in winter, so they can be prepared in advance.

For the actual ceremony, I made an arch rather like the frame of some beautiful Renaissance fresco. To complement the citrus theme, I entwined branches of laurel through a garden archway, adding oranges and binding it up with white ribbon. After the ceremony, long trestle tables were set up in these beautiful garden rooms with real kumquat plants—trained into miniature standard trees—placed along their lengths. Matching garlands were draped around the buffet tables and the bride and groom were then seated together under the matrimonial archway.

As the finishing touch, parterres were made at either side of the entrance using growing rosemary plants bedded in moss with orange-centered white crocus to continue the color scheme. Both can be replanted in the newlyweds' garden as a memento of their wedding day.

romantic

SIMPLE SPRING FLOWERS, such as the ones I used here, are too often overlooked by brides and florists alike. When they do make an appearance, it tends to be in oddly contorted "stylish" ways that destroy their innate sweetness. Their fairly short availability makes them even more appealing to me and, in the right context, they seem practically to arrange themselves with artless charm.

This wedding is just such a context. A wonderful trailing regency riding coat over an Empire line dress is an ingeniously successful update of historical fashion, and perfectly suits the ancient country church and garden setting. The subtle coloring of the bride's dress blends with the golden stone of the building, giving a perfect excuse—if excuse were needed—to explore color in the bridal flowers and in the other decorations.

A hat that vaguely resembled a Regency riding hat seemed the perfect choice for the bride. To make it really special, I filled the brim with lilies-of-the-valley and primroses, using the symbolism of the language of flowers—which was quite an obsession in the early nineteenth century—to combine appropriate messages of youthfulness, constancy, and happiness. The flowers were bound on to a circle of wire, made to fit around the crown of the hat, rather like an outsize headdress.

LEFT The bride's hat is trimmed with primroses and lilies-of-the-valley; she holds a satin purse combining the same with a few stems of auricula.
OPPOSITE A whole garden of forget-me-nots, primroses, and maidenhair ferns, with fritillaries (*Fritillaria persica*), bluebells, Solomon's seal, and trails of *Clematis montana* decorating the church porch.

The Empire Line

The language of flowers is spoken with the gloriously clean colors of spring at this large country wedding inspired by Jane Austen's best heroines. The flowers leave a satisfying impression of old-fashioned sweetness, charm, and simplicity.

CLOCKWISE FROM TOP LEFT A circlet of dainty sky-blue forget-me-nots (for remembrance) for the bridesmaid; and for the bride, primroses (for youth) and lilies-of-the-valley (for constancy and happiness); artless posies of cowslips, forget-me-nots, auriculas, primroses, bluebells, and pansies, in china cups adorn the tables; the bride's purse, with the same flowers as her hat, tones with the brocade of her dress.

By now I felt that a posy bouquet—albeit appropriate to the period—might detract from the rather quaint and dandified overall effect, so I came up with the idea of a satin drawstring purse filled with flowers to match the hat. I could not resist adding auriculas which toned so beautifully with the golden damask. I tied the flowers into a posy shape and placed the ends (wrapped in moist absorbent cotton) in a plastic cup fitted inside the purse.

Rather than give the bridesmaid matching flowers, I chose other spring treasures—pansies (for thoughts—from the French "pensée") and forget-me-nots (unsurprisingly, for remembrance). If all this seems too sentimental, then simply enjoy the flowers for their esthetic qualities. The tied posy combined both flowers while the circlet headdress comprised forget-me-nots (bound on to milliner's wire) with no extra foliage to dilute their unique blueness.

The chosen church could not have been more perfect for these old-fashioned flowers. The ledges in the porch were actually seats, but made perfectly proportioned bases for welcoming "gardens" of flowers. I combined living plants with cut blooms, and arranged them as if they were growing by gathering a generous sweep of one type of flower into a range of bowls and pots filled with wet florist's foam; I then hid these containers with moss or trailing ferns. The trails of clematis created the lightest suggestion of an archway without distracting from the superb carved stone. The principle is that the less hard one tries, the more successful this approach will be.

Inside the church, simplicity of both content and design continued to be the key. The refined delicacy and sheer scale of the sweeping floral pew ends created just the right feel in this very wide aisle. (In a narrow aisle these would be a waste of effort and a potentially dangerous obstruction!) I tend to avoid large traditional groups of flowers with this style of decoration, and would rather decorate window ledges to match the porch, or encircle column tops with trails of clematis and ferns, so that the use of tall, unseasonal flowers is completely unnecessary.

ABOVE If you must decorate the ends of church pews, make them dramatic. These ancient oak pews are lavishly decorated with a cascade of *Clematis montana*, arching stems of Solomon's seal (*Polygonatum*), fronds of maidenhair fern (*Adiantum capillus-veneris*), and bunches of primroses (*Primula vulgaris*), showing how simple, natural ingredients can have as much impact as expensive, unseasonal blooms when used well. They are all arranged in blocks of wet florist's foam secured in plastic cages, with a hook attached, and a hard plastic back designed to protect the wood from water damage.

Clean and classical

but still with an old-fashioned charm, this more understated version of the Regency theme is based on a green-and-white color palette and a smaller variety of spring flowers.

The early nineteenth-century interest in nature—albeit a highly pastoral, romanticized one—was matched by an equal fascination with classicism, and this is reflected both in the fashion and in the architecture of the time. If the romantic country idyll inspired the last few pages, this wedding reflects that more classical aspect.

The bridal dress is cut in the so-called "Empire-line" style which is so reminiscent of ancient Greek flowing but clinging gowns. This inspired the classical hairstyle and the delicate garland of Mexican orange blossom— a clever combination of Grecian style and a reference to the traditional bridal orange blossom. The bouquet is more regency than Grecian in style, with sprays of blossom tied with bunches of lily-of-the-valley, and ranunculus and other greenery, in a roughly circular posy shape. With these types of flowers, it is important to avoid a perfect circle: this would be difficult to achieve, in any case, with such flowing ingredients, and a failed perfect circle will always look far more amateurish than a more-messy-than-intended irregular shape!

The buffet-table decoration is pure classical revival, reminiscent of the plasterwork so popular in the period or of the painted borders on china plates. Clean laurel leaves make a garland which, combined with the other arrangements, epitomizes this wedding's blend of sophisticated classicism and romantic charm.

OPPOSITE AND ABOVE A mouth-watering green-and-white combination of ranunculus, lily-of-the-valley, Mexican orange blossom (*Choisya ternata*), and the sharp green bells of the unfortunately named stinking hellebore (*Helleborus foetidus*) is tied together with silk ribbon to create the bridal bouquet.

TOP RIGHT A buffet table decorated in a grand, Regency-inspired style: a formally draped garland of glossy, rich laurel leaves echoes the period's fascination with classicism. The leaves were attached to ribbon using a hot glue-gun and bent into shape as the length progressed. The finished garland was then pinned to the tablecloth. It is softened by the gentle posy of lily-of-the-valley; a stately silver epergne, generously filled with white bluebells, Solomon's seal (*Polygonatum*), and maidenhair fern (*Adiantum capillus-veneris*), gives height and raises the flowers above the level of the food.

RIGHT The profusion of the bouquet is tempered by this delicate garland of Mexican orange blossom, successfully masquerading as traditional orange blossom. The latter is, of course, the time-honored choice of brides, with obvious connotations of future fruitfulness, but this may be a more appropriate choice for the contemporary or less maternally inclined bride.

IN RECENT YEARS, romantic wedding fashions and flowers have had a bad press. The sumptuous "fairy princess" look of the 1980s has evolved into tailored sophistication but, just as there were many unfortunate victims of the "meringue" style then, so are there today as many ill-advised devotees of the tight and clinging look. The message—as ever—is that a bride should wear whatever suits her best.

Thus resolved to be more generously inclined toward the much maligned romantic bride, I set out to create a romantic floral look that actually did justice to its original inspiration. Fashions of the eighteenth century, like those of the Elizabethan era, have formed a rich fund of ideas for the designers of romantic wedding dresses. In the case of the former, results have ranged from the coy shepherdess bride to the brazen temptress emerging apparently almost naked from a frothing sea of a skirt: both these extremes seem rather *outré* today. Happily, however, there are still designers who are interpreting the era with the modern woman in mind. The opulent vanilla-colored silk brocade used for this dress would look at home in any painting of the period, and its voluptuous skirt and fitted, boned bodice definitely have an aura of the

LEFT The bridesmaid wears a circlet of Lenten hellebores (*Helleborus orientalis*), auriculas, lilac, individual hyacinth flowers, and sprigs of jasmine (*Jasminum polyanthum*).
OPPOSITE The wedding party in a garden bedecked with "garlands" of lilac, like one of Watteau's charmingly pastoral painted idylls.

Fête Champêtre

The eighteenth century inspires an idyllic but stylish wedding in the Arcadian vein, with armfuls of scented lilac and beribboned garlands of painterly flowers lending a romantic and evocative aura to the proceedings.

ABOVE The superb *croquembouche* wedding cake is placed upon a circular garland of lilac (*Syringa vulgaris*) in shades of lavender and amethyst. Like a mirror image above the cake, another larger garland is suspended on silken ribbons in palest aquamarine and gray from the overhanging branch of a tree. Both garlands were made on commercially produced circular wire wreath frames. Blocks of wet florist's foam were attached with green tape and disguised with sphagnum moss, then the lilac was arranged in generous quantities to give a solidity of color.

eighteenth century. The scooped décolletage and modest long sleeves cleverly combine shepherdess and *grande dame*, and this triggered an inspiring line of thought. The French eighteenth-century fabric called toile de Jouy often depicts idyllic rural scenes of romantic trysts and flowery bowers—just right for the relative plainness of this dress, and its context. So ideas for the flowers began to develop.

Garlands of flowers are a major feature of this toile fabric, as indeed they are in many eighteenth-century paintings. I decided that, rather than holding a bouquet, the bride could carry a delicate garland of flowers (as would her bridesmaid) and, instead of creating a solid rope of flowers, I made this ethereally light version. First of all, I entwined long trails of jasmine (cut from growing plants) and ribbon with a wire cut to the required finished length. I held the three components together at various points with short twists of fine wire, and then used a hot glue-gun to attach flower heads in clumps over these fixing points and singly along the length of the garland. It can seem rather daunting to use hot glue on delicate flowers, but in fact it seems to do more damage to florists' fingers than to flowers. Perhaps because the stalks are sealed and the flowers are handled less than when one wires them, they last perfectly well after this treatment—in fact I find that auriculas and hellebores last significantly longer.

The result is a much lighter, more whimsical garland than the usual effect using wired flowers, where extra flowers or greenery would be required to hide the wires. Such a garland could be used to link several bridesmaids, each could carry an individual garland, or a pair could hold one between them.

With neither the bride nor the bridesmaid carrying a bouquet, it was particularly important to choose styles of headdress that would not produce a top-heavy appearance. For the bride, I decided on this sweeping curve of flowers to echo the garland and to be worn discreetly at the back of the head where it looked in proportion to the other flowers.

ABOVE The bride's crescent-shaped headdress is attached at the back of her head as if actually holding the neat chignon in place. Its contents, too, were inspired by eighteenth-century flower paintings: purple-blotched hellebores, regal velvety auriculas, pink-tinged jasmine, white scented hyacinths, and clusters of lilac.

RIGHT A detail of the garland that gracefully links the bridesmaid and the bride. The choice of flowers continues in the eighteenth-century vein and includes these "parrot" or "baroque" tulips whose misshapen beauty drove many an eighteenth-century gardener into a passionate frenzy! The main garland is constructed on a fine wire and the delicate ribbons which appear to bind the whole arrangement together are, in fact, purely decorative.

LEFT This whimsically pastoral table arrangement is made in an upturned straw sunhat. I first painted it a delicate shade of green and then tied it "bonnet style" with a fine wire hidden by silk ribbon. The flowers are lilac and baroque tulips, with a few silvery sprigs of whitebeam (*Sorbus aria* 'Lutescens'), arranged in a bowl of wet florist's foam so that they cascade out of the hat without hiding its shape.

The circlet headdress, another frequent prop in eighteenth-century paintings and depicted on toile de Jouy, was the perfect and traditional choice for the young bridesmaid. I tried to make the headdresses as airy and delicate as possible by using both wire and a glue-gun to attach the individual flowers.

Rarely do flowers seem appropriate for pageboys at a wedding, but in this case I copied an idea from a painting, and these flowers on a stick seemed to add the perfect finishing touch to the page's courtly golden jacket and green velvet sash.

The reception was to be held in a large informal garden, so it seemed important to find a way of delineating the party area and creating a festive look, while refraining from imposing unsuitably grand floral decorations on what was otherwise an unpretentious setting. The idea of hanging garlands was once again drawn straight from source: characters illustrated in toile de Jouy frequently have such garlands suspended over them. The magnificent *croquembouche* wedding cake was decorated in exactly this way, making it absolutely perfect for its garden setting. The idea for the avenue of birch poles with hanging garlands arose from necessity, namely, to direct the guests through the garden. It is an adaptation of the cake decoration that is both beautiful and functional, and helps to unify the whole floral scheme.

It would perhaps have been a little excessive to use smaller lilac garlands on the tables as well, so I invented these charmingly rustic arrangements in inexpensive upturned sunhats—again very much in keeping with the spirit of the whole wedding. These sunhats are easy to find in stores which sell baskets, rope, and raffia.

For another occasion, it might be tempting to decorate the tables with white lilac, or with white roses, garlanded upon tablecloths of black-and-white toile de Jouy. Indeed, this could be the starting point for an ultra-chic, black-and-white version of these wedding flowers, or possibly an interesting alternative for seasons when such an exquisite range of garden flowers is unavailable.

One could also adapt the hanging-garland idea to decorate the poles in a marquee, especially if there were difficult color schemes to contend with. Garlands of white daisies hung from navy velvet ribbons, for example, would look much more exciting than the more obvious daisy-and-cornflower mixture.

TOP LEFT The avenue of lilac garlands, suspended from beribboned birch poles, meanders through the garden, lending a sense of structure and formality to the setting, as well as providing a romantic way of directing wedding guests to the terrace where tables are laid for dinner. **ABOVE AND LEFT** The pageboy's stick of flowers provides a rare opportunity for a boy to carry flowers. The idea was copied from a painting of the goddess Flora in which her young male attendant holds an identical arrangement, and was made by binding lilac, jasmine, hellebores, auriculas, and tulips to the top of a short pole. The stems of the flowers, and the pole, were neatly concealed with ribbon.

The alluring, sensual

side of the eighteenth century is interpreted here with jewel-like flowers for the bride and voluptuous arrangements inspired by the great flower paintings of the era.

ABOVE Again I have chosen these rather "antique" flowers for this elegant sweep of a headdress which sensuously outlines the curve of the bride's formal, upswept hairstyle. Rather than the clear pinks and purples of the previous page, I have picked unusual "muddy" colors, inspired by faded old needlepoint–dull sandy gold, taupe, greens, and grays–with a hint of strong purple in the centers of the hellebores and auriculas. A hot glue-gun was used to attach the flower heads to a shaped piece of wire covered in green florist's tape. For some reason, both auriculas and hellebores seem to prefer this to being wired, and last perfectly for at least a day with their stems sealed by the hot glue.

There is another aspect of the eighteenth century which is the antithesis, in some ways, of the rural romance evoked on the preceding pages. The world of the aristocracy, so vividly portrayed in films such as *Amadeus* or *Les Liaisons Dangereuses*, was one of sensual decadence and courtly flirtations. Dresses were designed both to flatter and to reveal—another trend that recurs in many contemporary wedding dresses.

If a bride has chosen such a sensual style of dress, I feel that it is pointless feigning modesty with demure bouquets and coy circlets. Equally, the frequent alternative—outrageous colors and voluptuous quantities of flowers—can easily reduce sensuality to vulgarity, which is a great pity. For this type of dress I prefer to design flowers to be worn as pieces of delicate jewelry, much as they were in many eighteenth-century paintings. Somehow this gives an air of dignity to what was, in that era, a very acceptable degree of exposure. It makes the dress look more like a lavish ball gown than a skimpy wedding dress.

This bridal headdress was based on an eighteenth-century tiara belonging to the Danish royal family. It coils closely around the bride's head, from a fine point at the nape of her neck to a wider band on the crown. It is essential to experiment in advance with this sort of shape as the result is generally a collaboration between hairdresser and florist; making a trial version in silk or old dried flowers is a good idea. The faded colors chosen here contribute to the sophisticated end-product.

A bouquet of flowers would, I feel, spoil the allure of this style so instead I made this interesting corsage, to be tucked into the bride's cleavage. The flowers were wired individually and bound into a single stem, fixed to the bodice under this gray silk ribbon.

What could be more appropriate to decorate the room than a still-life of flowers, the fashionable commission of many aristocrats of the period? Often an artist was instructed to paint the rarest, most sought-after flowers—placed nonchalantly amongst country blooms—as a public demonstration of a patron's access to both.

LEFT A beautiful eighteenth-century flower painting is brought to life. In this interpretation of the genre, I used mostly garden flowers arranged in a silvery urn. These included hellebores, globe artichokes, creamy cherry blossom (*Prunus* 'Ukon'), viburnum (*V. x burkwoodii* and *V. opulus*), foxgloves, flag iris, Solomon's seal (*Polygonatum*), centaurea, euphorbia (*E. characias* subsp. *wulfenii*), fritillaries (*F. meleagris* and *F. persica*), and alliums.

ABOVE Fine eighteenth-century ladies often used flowers in place of jewelry and, with crazes like "tulipomania," they were probably more valuable! This pinned corsage manages to preserve modesty and make a novel alternative to a bouquet when worn with a sensual and elaborate dress. Using rather odd colors, it combines intensely desirable tulips and auriculas with the more common hellebores and snake's-head fritillaries (*F. meleagris*.)

IT IS FASCINATING to take a nostalgic look back at the styles of clothing and flowers that were in vogue at the beginning of the twentieth century, the so-called "Belle Epoque," a time of exquisite fashions and wicked decadence. The heavy primness of high Victorian tastes and lifestyles was being replaced by a youthful lightness and *joie de vivre*. Photographs of society weddings of the period show tightly corseted dresses with daringly plunging necklines, long gloves to preserve modesty, and huge bouquets which obscure almost everything else!

This dress is reminiscent of turn-of-the-century afternoon dresses—mercifully less corseted than their evening counterparts—but with the evening-style décolletage. Its utter simplicity immediately gives it a contemporary twist, but it was the romantic, period aspect that I decided to emphasize. The ensemble has an old-fashioned charm but is lighter and more attractive to today's bride than an accurate copy might have been.

Garden roses seemed the perfect flower on which to base the whole scheme. They have that blowzy summery look which is so evocative of long Edwardian afternoons, and trails of roses make superlative long bouquets. The shape of this elegant sweep of flowers was inspired by the beautifully draped chiffon bodice. More

LEFT A perfect romantic vision: elements borrowed from the early twentieth century, adapted to give a fresh, elegant look for today.
OPPOSITE The bride's hair is scooped into this latticed snood of pearl-edged ribbon and trimmed with delicate sprays of creamy roses and lilies-of-the-valley for a graceful and sophisticated style.

La Belle Epoque

Decadence and delicacy combine in the flowers for this romantic contemporary wedding. The whole scheme borrows rather than copies and the result is a light, fresh version of a traditional style with an air of aristocratic refinement.

asymmetrical and natural-looking than the traditional downward-pointing shower shape, it was a conscious simplification of the huge, heavy bouquets that would have been in vogue then. This degree of lightness and airiness was achieved by wiring the flowers and keeping large solid blooms only in the center with small delicate sprays at the extremities. The roses are combined with lilies-of-the-valley—very popular at the time—and trails of sweet-smelling honeysuckle.

It can be difficult to adapt a modern hairstyle to a period-style dress—often people do not even try—but it is important to balance the mood of the dress if a unified whole is the aim. This bride's snood is a simple way of giving an illusion of greater volume to the hair, and also controls short layers. I made it by twisting pearl-edged wired ribbon and stitching the intersections. Two graceful sprays of flowers curve up and around the head, creating an elegant crescent shape.

The bridesmaid's roses were intentionally less delicate than those of the bride. A tied bunch combined roses in shades of pink and gold—a strong, modern color contrast which prevented any tendency toward excessive sweetness. The large hat was crowned with an exuberant garland of the same roses—romantic and yet, with the plain, boat-necked dress, rather simple and chic.

Floral decorations for the ceremony and reception needed to combine this delicacy and exuberance. The silver epergnes made wonderful table decorations, the slender stems giving a lightness to the flowers at the top.

TOP LEFT The shape of the sweeping bridal bouquet echoes the draped chiffon of the bodice and, being wired, is the epitome of visual and physical lightness, a vital consideration if a large bouquet is to avoid looking clumsy. In the language of flowers it incorporates English roses 'Francine Austin' and 'The Pilgrim' for love, trails of honeysuckle to denote devotion, and sweet-smelling lilies-of-the-valley for happiness—a message that is uniquely and universally appealing.

LEFT The cake table groans under the weight of its flowers. Again English roses are used, with trails of ivy pinned along the front of the table and climbing the cake itself in a romantic overgrown style. Two silver epergnes, brimming with roses and sweet peas, balance the cake's height.

OPPOSITE The bridesmaid's picture hat is trimmed with English roses, 'Sharifa Asma', 'The Pilgrim', 'Jude the Obscure', and 'Golden Celebrations', with a simple posy of the same flowers.

Black and white

is an unusual choice of color for a wedding gown, but the effect is striking when combined with densely packed white flowers fashioned into a small tiara headdress with an exuberantly large bouquet or a tiny old-fashioned posy.

ABOVE The essential accessory for any woman in the last century, a posy-holder, makes a beautiful gift for a romantic bride today. As an alternative to the large bouquet, the stylized delicacy of this posy makes it the ideal partner to the quirky tiara. Here, I simply tied polyantha roses together before placing them in the silver holder and securing it with a silver pin. Flowers for these holders should not be too big or the delicate proportions of the holder will be obscured.

In the film of the musical *My Fair Lady,* there is a gloriously decorative scene set at Ascot races. It was designed by Cecil Beaton using a monochrome color scheme—a daring *coup de théâtre* in a film made in color, at a time when black-and-white films were still being made frequently. This wedding dress has a similar élan and daring, black being a color rarely associated with weddings. Again, it has a definite period feel and the exquisitely ornate embroidery emphasizes this.

It would have been a shame to break the chiaroscuro effect by adding any color, so I decided to use clouds of white flowers—with the barest hint of green simply to stop them looking artificial. I made a large bouquet of frothy white peonies and rose trails, which echoed the roses embroidered in jet on the dress. For a headdress, I made a dainty tiara, again inspired by Cecil Beaton's designs for *My Fair Lady.* It is definitely of the stylized school of floristry and the roses appear almost artificial in their uncharacteristic symmetry, but utterly charming nonetheless. The effect could be repeated with other small regular-shaped flowers, or even berries.

As far as decorations for the reception are concerned, what could be more perfect than ornate black wire baskets, piled with luscious white roses or hydrangeas?

"*Eliza, who is exquisitely dressed, produces an impression of such remarkable distinction and beauty as she enters that they all rise, quite fluttered.*"

George Bernard Shaw *Pygmalion*

ABOVE The bride wears a tiny tiara headdress of tightly packed flowers—again, polyantha roses. The blooms were first wired into graduated spikes, which were then attached to a wire base which could be secured behind and under the small topknot of hair.

RIGHT The bride carries a glorious bouquet of puff-ball white peonies with asymmetrical trails of roses. As with the headdress, the bouquet was wired to create volume without weight. Its whiteness—almost undiluted by green—is particularly flattering to the sharp contrasts of the unusual black-and-white wedding gown.

GONE ARE THE DAYS when a romantic wedding dress involved yards of lace and dozens of bewildered bows. Today's designers are still creating gowns that spell pure romance, yet with lines and fabrics of exquisite refinement. Flowers to accompany such dresses need an equally simple approach. Overabundance can be avoided by using perhaps only one or two types of flower, and by toning down a mixture of colors to a softer blend of similar hues.

This dress epitomizes the best modern romantic wedding gowns. The almost gray-white organza of the full skirt and modest bodice is warmed in the subtlest way by the barest pink blush in the pleated satin sash. To me, its colors and textures demanded the gentlest of flowers and yet its striking simplicity deserved an equally strong floral statement rather than something merely pretty. It is easy to forget that flowers are pretty in themselves—we do not need to help them—indeed, trying to create a "pretty" effect often hides this natural beauty in contrivance.

I chose this garden rose as the starting point for these wedding flowers. Its open-centered fullness seemed to match the floating organza skirts in both texture and voluptuousness, while the subtle coloring—blush-touched ivory—echoed the delicacy of the dress.

LEFT A few well-chosen blooms of the deliciously scented *Rosa* 'Margaret Merril', a simple, elegant decoration for a classic chignon.
OPPOSITE To complete the picture, a romantic bouquet of the same roses with sprays of the white 'Iceberg' rose complements the gray whites of the organza and blush pink of the satin to perfection.

Simply Romantic

The elegant combination of romantic fabrics and gentle colors in this ethereal dress demands the lightest touch in any accompanying flowers. These roses both complete the picture and complement the dress, providing impact with natural beauty and simplicity.

CLOCKWISE FROM TOP LEFT

A perfect single rose; blown roses, blush, green, and ivory hydrangeas, and trails of ivy are garlanded around a stone candleholder which prevents triteness in this opulent table decoration; pastel hues continue with sugared almonds in pretty organza purses; the silvery tint of the rue in the bridesmaids' posies echoes the gray solidity of the stonework.

I decorated a classic chignon with four open blooms for the simplest and most elegant of bridal headdresses. Each was individually wired, and the wire ends were used like hairclips to anchor the roses firmly in the hair. Wiring with florist's tape ensures that the ends of the stems are sealed, so that the flowers lose less moisture and last longer. For the bouquet, I added the starker white 'Iceberg' rose, to complement the whiteness of the skirts and provide variety without adding another type of flower.

The typical romantic bouquet comprises a collection of different flowers. This simpler, rather more sophisticated, version was made by choosing one species of flower, but combining different colors, degrees of openness, or types to provide variety. Again, the flowers were wired to create a loose irregular shape. Such an effect is impossible to achieve with tied posies, as the flowers must be held in place either with foliage or with more tightly packed flowers.

Tiny bridesmaids were given circlets of flowers for their hair in slightly stronger shades of pink. I used commercial rather than garden roses, as they are easier to find in quantity. The bridal roses were echoed in blooms of the rose 'Hester', but by adding miniature roses, delicate rue, and hydrangeas, the effect was scaled down to suit tiny heads. To complement the headdresses, the same flowers were tied into posies.

For the tables, I constructed generous circular garlands from open commercial roses in ice-cream shades rather than the more obvious pink. I used some old stone balustrades—to be found at architectural reclamation yards or garden centers—as central candleholders. These helped to create an appropriately fairytale atmosphere while lending a sense of structure and solidity to the ethereal roses.

For a spring wedding, the same effect could be created by replacing the roses with double tulips which have a similar fullness and diaphanous quality. The blush white tulip 'Angelique', for instance, could be teamed with clusters of 'Paper White' narcissi on the table to give exquisite scent and variety of texture.

ABOVE The bridesmaids' tulle skirts match the bride's floating organza. The large open roses in their circlets are a pinker version of hers and these are teamed with pretty miniature roses, tiny clusters of hydrangeas, and delicate rue to give them a child-like feel. Matching posies are tied with white satin ribbons.

MANY OF THE ELEMENTS of contemporary romantic wedding dresses are drawn from the Elizabethan era: corseted and laced tops above billowing skirts, pointed bodices, and off-the-shoulder necklines. However, this historical inspiration is seldom extended to the choice of flowers and the style of decoration.

Given a gown of ivory chiffon with an embroidered gold corset top, I tried to find a sympathetic look for the wedding flowers. Influenced by the season, I chose a palette that might be found in an antique tapestry—coppery reds, golds, russets, and warm browns with soft grays, blues, and purples. These all harmonized with the warm brick of the Elizabethan country house and chapel in the fall landscape that formed the setting for the wedding. As with all historical themes, the aim was to capture the flavor of the period, rather than striving slavishly for an "authentic" look.

For the bridal bouquet I designed a large tied sheaf of flowers to be carried over one arm. Unsophisticated and yet romantic, the style is perfect for this dress, whereas it might look unwieldy with a slimline, elegant ensemble. Using my hand like a container, I first made a rough outline with stems of oak, softened it with the trailing stephanandra, and, lastly, added the richly hued

LEFT Carved wooden candle niches are backed by a glowing tapestry of fall oak leaves—traditionally used at weddings to signify the strength of love—held in place by red-blushed golden pears.
OPPOSITE The bride carries an abundant sheaf of fall leaves, trails of stephanandra, and rich bronze, apricot, and gold hybrid sunflowers.

Elizabethan

The muted colors of Elizabethan tapestries inspired the decorations for this romantic wedding on a grand scale. Full use is made of fall's bounty, perfectly reiterating the soft colors of the surrounding countryside.

PREVIOUS PAGE LEFT (clockwise from top left) The colors of the flowers were inspired by antique tapestries. The bridal headdress, made of metallic hydrangeas, fall leaves, silvery rue, and lavender; an archway of pale green eucalyptus, mottled bronze beech, crabapples, golden oakleaves, and hydrangeas at the church entrance; and the bridesmaid's headdress and pomander, again using steely bluish-green hydrangeas, echinops, thyme, eucalyptus, and hypericum berries. PREVIOUS PAGE RIGHT A glorious archway at the church entrance establishes the fall color palette for the wedding. It is made from golden beech leaves, copper oak and maple leaves, silver eucalyptus, and the burgundy reds of sedum, hydrangea, and crabapple. LEFT Long tables decorated with "garlands" of scented herbs, echinops, sedum crabapple, and copper beech, arranged in long trays of wet florist's foam and punctuated by pewter platters of symmetrically piled pomegranates to add color and variety of texture.

sunflowers. The stems were then tied with strong green string and placed in a jug of cool water. At the last minute, they were lifted out, dried, and the string hidden by a swag of brocade or ribbon. It is important that this type of large bouquet looks as though it is held in a relaxed fashion. Rather than clutching it high on the arm, the bride should opt for a lower position.

A large bridal headdress was needed to balance the scale of this bouquet, but I wanted to avoid creating a huge "swimming cap" of flowers. Instead, I borrowed the shape of the cloth halo headdresses that I had seen in paintings of the period, and copied its height simply with large leaves trimmed delicately with smaller flowers.

I made a similar top-of-head decoration for the bridesmaid, but with ribbons from each end fastened to hold it securely in place. She carried a "pomander"— hung with a tassel from a silken carrying rope—made by wiring flowers individually and pushing them into a small, tightly bound ball of moss in a regular compact pattern. Equally, one could wire or glue flowers to a

storebought pre-formed ball. Leftover wired flower-and-leaf clusters were bound to some ribbon and, in a gesture totally in keeping with the historic theme, tied as floral collars for a pair of stone greyhounds—much more effective than ribbons on gates or more traditional flower arrangements, which never look right outdoors.

I created a lavish archway over the church door to introduce the autumnal feeling, fastening the flowers in wet florist's foam covered in chicken wire and secured at intervals around the door frame. I did not continue it to ground level, both to avoid obscuring the beautiful wood and to keep it from looking too heavy and earthbound.

The narrow tables chosen for the evening dinner may be suitable for the period, but they are notoriously difficult to decorate successfully. While rows of small arrangements look mean, long arrangements can look like battleships sailing through a channel. A continuous garland of fruit, foliage, and herbs running down the middle of the table made an elegant alternative, with platters of pomegranates added at intervals to provide variation in height and blocks of color on the rich damask cloths.

Garlands like these would be equally effective and apposite for a spring wedding, using banks of miniature daffodils or narcissus; while summer's richly colored garden roses would also make a glorious alternative.

LEFT AND BELOW The subtle, unexpected side of fall: a graceful bridal bouquet designed around a few magical blooms of the autumn-flowering climber *Cobaea scandens*. The other ingredients are trails of honeysuckle, sprays of snowberry, green hydrangea, vine leaves, and a few late buds of *Hydrangea paniculata*.

OPPOSITE The bride's veil is held in place by a snug Juliet cap constructed entirely of snowberries wired in tiny clusters and bound to an open wire shape made to fit her head.

Pure and simple:

the alternative but dazzling face of fall in simple whites and greens. The bride wears a delicate Juliet cap of snowberries, that is inspired by Queen Elizabeth I's legendary passion for pearls.

The perennial appeal of simple white-and-green color schemes for wedding flowers never seems to diminish. Even in the riotous mêlée of most fall gardens, filled with their hues of gold, brown, and red, there are often a few hidden treasures which make the appeal of a calmer palette wholly justified. For me, one such treasure is the flower of the climbing annual *Cobea scandens* 'Alba'— also known by its common name, the cup-and-saucer vine, a perfect description of its flower shape. Here, a handful of these blooms forms the basis of an exquisite wired wedding bouquet that seems utterly suited to the Elizabethan age with its trails of scented honeysuckle and pearl-like snowberries. It is easy to make this light and elegant style using outlining sprays of honeysuckle and hydrangea, keeping the bulkier berries and flowers for the center.

To complement the bouquet, I designed a very special headdress, a pointed Juliet cap made solely of snowberries. I made it by firstly molding the basic shape in milliner's wire which was then adjusted to fit the bride's head. Several crossbands were added and the whole thing bound with tiny wired clusters of snowberries. Again, a hot glue-gun could be used to speed the process, but it might perhaps result in a more fragile headdress. Whatever the method used, the result is exquisite and

jewel-like but at the same time unpretentious and youthful. It is a good idea to wire a few extra clusters of berries to add in case you notice any gaps once the headdress is in place.

For a simple room or church decoration, the perfect flowers to complement the white-and-green color scheme of this stylish fall wedding would be longi lilies. In late medieval paintings lilies were always arranged vertically, as they were symbolic of the offering up of prayers. Table decorations could combine longi lilies with sprays of snowberries and some green foliage just beginning to show its fall colors arranged in rusty metal urns.

DECORATIONS AT CHRISTMAS usually include a surplus of rich dark evergreens and, indeed, many Christmas weddings are memorably decorated in this way. Others have fun as their main ingredient, and adopt a bright, fun theme. The light and glowing approach of this Christmas wedding had its roots in the most ancient symbolism of the season—the appearance of light in darkness—and I tried to adapt this in a clean, elegant, and yet romantic way.

The plain setting of this ivory-painted, vaulted room and the almost vestment-like wedding dress were perfect starting points, so I felt inspired from the outset. Taking light as my primary focus throughout, I interpreted it with the simple palette of a few white winter flowers, glowing cream or golden clothes, and gilt touches to catch the twinkling candlelight. Greenery was kept to a minimum.

For the bride's bouquet I used a singularly appropriate white flower, the Christmas rose, against a background of dark green fir branches and, by wiring all the ingredients, created a loose and natural look.

The bride's headdress is a floral *trompe-l'oeil*: the floral chignon is actually hollow. It consists of several interwoven wires bound with individually wired flowers

LEFT The Christmas rose (*Helleborus niger*), its waxy cream petals and golden stamens the perfect partner for the heavy ivory damask of the bride's dress, is combined with buds of *Skimmia japonica* and various types of fir and fir cones in her natural-looking bouquet.
OPPOSITE Scented hyacinths adorn the candlelit dinner tables.

A Christmas Wedding

This Christmas wedding is a feast of romantic golden light. Candles surround the room and spill over the tables where scented rings of white hyacinths echo the clustered hyacinths and simple Christmas roses of the bridal party.

and foliage—a time-consuming exercise but I can think of no simpler equivalent. It could equally well be made to fit over a chignon of real hair.

The bridesmaids' dresses were modeled on the robes of Venetian choirboys in an eighteenth-century painting, but the real fur trim on their cuffs and around the matching velvet brocade skullcaps was replaced by bands of hyacinth flowers sewn on to these cuffs and headdresses. The effect is both charming and practical. Small bridesmaids have nothing to drop, and older bridesmaids have their hands free to help the bride. The hyacinth flowers can either be individually wired and bound on to a single wire, or glued to a wide ribbon, but the latter is more delicate and therefore less likely to withstand severe wear and tear.

OPPOSITE (clockwise from top left)
The creamy damask of the bride's buttoned coat contrasts beautifully with the Christmas roses' golden stamens; the gold is continued in the velvet of the bridesmaid's flower-trimmed choirboy robes, their cuffs encircled with hyacinth flowers; bowls of floating candles on the tables cast pools of light and shadow on to the gilt organza cloth; the golden-haired little bridesmaid wears a simple, scented skullcap.
ABOVE The overall view of the room: the walls are punctuated by candelabra and the niches filled with stone urns of fir branches, hung with twinkling lanterns to give a sense of grandeur without ostentation.

The room was decorated with great simplicity. Large metal candelabra were used to give both height and light, while stone urns, filled with great branches of pine and fir, then hung with glass lanterns, made elegant and restrained floral statements.

The tables were a feast of light. Storm lanterns were each surrounded by a circlet of scented white hyacinths set in a ring of soaked florist's foam, trimmed with moss and short branches of pine and fir, while floating candles in two ribbed glass bowls of water on the tables created pools of ever-moving light on the golden gauze tablecloths. Night-lights, dotted around the room, lifted the scene into the realms of romance.

At either side of stone steps leading into the room, I made a bank of growing hyacinth and narcissus. This is one of the most effective ways of enhancing an architectural feature. Plants were simply arranged and pots hidden with moss. The flowers can be planted afterward as a lasting memory of the special day.

For a spring wedding, welcoming banks of daffodils or narcissi could be used like this and, in summer, marguerites banked on steps or along ledges in a church give an air of great simplicity. Alternatively, flowering rose plants could be entwined into a bower in a porch or used to lighten a dark corridor, complemented by a rosebud version of this floral chignon.

"... she felt as if her 'fun' had really begun at last, for the mirror had plainly told her that she was 'a little beauty'."

Louisa M. Alcott *Little Women*

TOP LEFT The bride's headdress is an exquisite chignon of flowers and foliage, an ideal choice for hair that is too short to be worn up.

LEFT An alternative version of the bride's wired bouquet: here the same ingredients are tied with gold ribbon into a smaller, more compact shape to create a more contemporary version of its romantic counterpart.

ABOVE The bridegroom's buttonhole consists of a few Christmas roses wired with sprigs of pine and a single ivy leaf.

MANY LARGE WEDDINGS TODAY have several components which all need to be given due consideration when deciding upon the flowers. The ceremony, a small luncheon, a large elegant dinner, and an evening dance may all take place within the space of a few hours. On these occasions, particularly, because they are expected to grace every stage of the celebrations with equal aplomb, the flowers work best when designed around a theme.

Here, with just such a wedding in mind, my starting-points were the bridal gown and its setting. The elegant Empire line dress and wonderful ivory velvet cloak seemed to come straight from the pages of a Tolstoy novel, while the grand country house, set in a winter landscape, conjured up romantic images of imperial Russian palaces and hunting lodges. However, it would have been neither appropriate nor clever to recreate a stage set fit for the characters of *Anna Karenina*. To be effective, I needed to use a more subtle touch.

The unusual bridal dress and cloak required an equally individual headdress, especially as there was no veil. The traditional Russian headdress, called a *kokoshnik* (literally meaning a cockscomb), was worn by peasants and grand duchesses alike, making it an ideal choice for this Russian-themed wedding. It was

LEFT The bride wears a tiara headdress made of snowdrops, its shape a modified version of the traditional Russian headdress—the *kokoshnik*.
OPPOSITE The bridesmaids wear the same style of headdress but made of brocade with a trim of snowdrops, wax-flowers, and blush anemones at the back. They carry small tied posies of the same flowers.

A Russian Romance

Russia's imperial past is the inspiration for this large winter wedding; the jewels of Fabergé recalled in delicate shades of pearl, pale amethyst, and rose for the daytime, with richer purples and golds lending an air of opulence and grandeur to the evening celebrations.

LEFT Elegant and intricate table arrangements for the luncheon tables are inspired by the work of Fabergé: a small glass bowl in a metal stand is filled with a delicate bunch of lily-of-the-valley (*Convallaria majalis*). Similar metal stands with glass containers are available in many department stores. I covered the legs with ruscus leaves in a regular pattern using a hot glue-gun. When set, these were lightly sprayed gold. The stand was then placed in a saucer of wet florist's foam mounded with anemones, wax-flowers, and more snowdrops, maintaining once again the link with the bridal flowers.
OPPOSITE The snowdrop (*Galanthus nivalis*) gives a sense of unity to the bridal entourage, appearing in the bridesmaids' posies and headdresses, and emerging as the star of the bride's magnificent floral tiara.

made of many things—from fabric to diamonds—and indeed is the origin of the tiara that we know today. I created a headdress that resembled the *kokoshnik* in both style and shape, made entirely from snowdrops. It was a time-consuming labor of love, and not for the impatient, but well worth the effort.

The basic structure was made from strong stub-wires (available from any florist's supplier), covered in florist's tape, then formed into two crescents and joined with several graduated wire uprights to make a hollow inverted "smile" shape. It is essential that this fits the bride's head, sitting at an angle which flatters both her features and hairstyle, so experiment well in advance. When the shape has been established, the flowers can be attached—preferably on the morning of the wedding to ensure that they last. Small clusters of snowdrops are wired and taped, and these are bound on to graduated

straight wires cut to fit the crescent outline. When each wire is full of snowdrop clusters, it can be attached with fine wire in its allotted slot on the crescent. Once completed, the headdress should be covered with moistened tissue paper until needed. It is a sensible idea to prepare a few extra clusters of snowdrops in case any gaps appear when it is actually in place.

With such a striking headdress, a simple posy of snowdrops would have made the perfect matching bouquet but, for a more dramatic effect, a muff of dark ivy leaves or fur, with a central cluster of snowdrops, would be equally appropriate.

It seemed a good idea to give the bridesmaids similar headdresses, but I decided to create these in the same ivory brocade as their dress sashes. Made to fit right around the head and then fastened with a large flat golden gauze bow at the back, these were decorated

CLOCKWISE FROM TOP LEFT

Shades of imperial purple and gold for the evening. The black horse pulling the couple's carriage is given a "plume" of hyacinths, wax-flower, and snowdrops; more gilded ruscus leaves around purple hyacinths, wax-flowers, anemones, and snowdrops on the tables; a delicate anemone; domes of tulips linked with gilt garlands decorate a grand staircase.

at the last possible moment with wired clusters of snowdrops, wax-flowers, and large, open anemones pushed straight into the hair.

The bridesmaids' small tied posies are made of the same flowers, finished with ivory silk bows. Basically warm whites and sepia, they delicately complement the golden gauze of their skirts. Snowdrops tie the scheme together, linking the bride and her bridesmaids.

The room for luncheon, with its gilded, delicately painted panels, demanded an equally sensitive choice of flowers. Being a tall room, it also required height on at least some of the tables. With the exquisite work of the Russian court jeweler Carl Fabergé as inspiration, I devised an ornate table arrangement combining these attributes. Stands of gilded leaves with trailing garlands draped across the table were placed over mounded arrangements of anemones, wax-flowers, and snowdrops, and the small glass container at the top was filled with out-of-season lilies-of-the-valley; this rather extravagant gesture seemed wholly appropriate for a scheme inspired by an opulent imperial court.

For the evening reception and dance, the bride, without cape and exchanging her snowdrops for a real tiara, struck an altogether more glamorous note. I think it can be quite fun to transform the innocent, exquisite image of the day into a more sophisticated adult look in the evening, and a simple bouquet of orchids, tinted with imperial purple, seemed perfect. Orchids sit well with an elaborate, sparkling tiara and, as well as being easy to carry throughout the evening, will stay fresh-looking.

Purple tones set a stronger theme for the night's festivities. An imposing entrance staircase was given massive domed finials of tulips in every regal shade of purple, lilac, and rose, linked with garlands of gilded magnolia leaves. These garlands echo the luncheon-table decorations and also form the basis of elegant candlelit evening versions with their circular gilded candelabra placed around a central arrangement of purple-toned anemones, purple hyacinths, wax-flowers, and the ubiquitous flower of the day—the snowdrop.

ABOVE The bride, replacing the tiara of snowdrops with a real tiara for the evening festivities, carries an equally glamorous bouquet composed of three cattleya orchids, veined and flushed with yellow and lilac, as if fresh from some imperial St Petersburg hothouse. Sprigs of wax-flower and trailing gauze ribbons soften the effect.

Velvety purple

African violets make a brilliant alternative choice for a smaller winter wedding, and look truly contemporary against the white fur of the bridal hat.

Overtones of imperial Russia are retained here, albeit more simply, for this small romantic wedding. The bride chose a plain white silk suit trimmed with fur and teamed it with a matching hat. African violets seemed to me to be the perfect complement to the soft fur, and contrasted with the pale color. While the purple-white combination is strikingly contemporary, the violet shade gives the scheme an old-fashioned feel to charming effect; the ribbons used to tie the posy add a further dimension to the romantic image. The whole ensemble would be perfect for a simple wedding where the couple is married by a judge.

Tables for a lunch or dinner afterward could be decorated with glass bowls of dark purple tulips on white linen. Alternatively, pots of growing African violets would make a simple and economical decoration, whatever the setting. Having established such a strong color combination in the bridal flowers, it would seem a shame to use flowers of another color to decorate the venue. Obviously, in the depths of winter, it might be difficult to find tall purple flowers, but you could, for example, use tall white flowers in a container decorated with purple velvet.

Common sweet violets (*Viola odorata*) would be the obvious choice of posy for a white spring suit, but equally beautiful would be a handful of lilies-of-the-valley (a great favorite of Fabergé) or primroses. Either would look exquisite as trimming for a white hat.

ABOVE The perfect blending of contemporary taste and old traditions: purple African violets have been wired and densely packed together into this molded, globe-shaped posy. It is tied with rich violet velvet ribbon, recalling the wedding bouquets of Russia's grand duchesses.

OPPOSITE A white fur cossack hat is given a living jewel of velvety African violets cut straight from the plant, wired into small clusters, and then shaped into this striking half-crescent.

alternative

STARKLY MODERN SURROUNDINGS may not be to everyone's taste for this most traditional of days, but they open another range of possibilities for the floral decorator. A space like this is a bare canvas, so an extravagant themed event is often chosen to disguise the blankness. If, however, you approach such a venue with the same acute eye for appropriateness that you might apply to a more historical setting, you can achieve equally interesting and perhaps even more striking results.

This glass-roofed art gallery, originally an old warehouse, has a rare sense of space for a city venue, and the quality of natural light that fills it is unique. The architect who designed the conversion obviously set out to enhance these characteristics and the result is a minimalist-style space with an emphasis on light.

In keeping with the setting, the bridal dress is an equally light, white organza coat worn over a column of silk—rather like a vestment and devoid of extraneous detail. Continuing with this approach, I decided that the bride should carry a single stem of camellia. This also fulfils all the requirements of the traditional bridal bouquet: it is a flower that can be held in the hand, looks exquisite, and enhances the whole ensemble in a way that a bunch of mixed flowers never could.

LEFT A perfect white camellia bloom makes a startlingly effective "bouquet" surrounded by its own richly lacquered green leaves.
OPPOSITE With their dove gray leaves just emerging, lofty branches of whitebeam (*Sorbus aria* 'Lutescens') make a striking impact in the uncluttered spaciousness of this modern room.

Minimalism

The scope of minimalism—the reduction of design to its essential elements—is explored here in the flowers for a city wedding. Far from diminishing the impact, simplicity and an emphasis on the flowers' individual qualities create a surprisingly dramatic effect.

LEFT A single stem of eucharis in a pyramidal glass vase makes a stylishly sculptural table decoration. Its height and exotic beauty make comparison with restaurant bud-vases unlikely.
OPPOSITE The single camellia of the "bouquet" is repeated in the bride's hair, wired and held in place by twisting the wire behind the unpretentious braid. Both flowers should be picked at the very last moment, and then kept in damp tissue until needed.

The bride's hair was worn in a simple thick braid to show off its best qualities—length and lustrous shine. It also gave me the opportunity to repeat the single camellia flower motif. The camellia is ideal for this treatment because it does not rely on bulk to look elegant. Indeed, over-generous arrangers can sometimes reduce it to an uncharacteristic "fluffiness."

There was a natural progression from the bride's flowers to the decorations on the tables at the wedding lunch. Again, I wanted to use a single perfect bloom on each table but was anxious to avoid a restaurant bud-vase scenario. Adding height seemed to be the solution but this ruled out more camellias, as single flowers are short stemmed and branches are both difficult to find and inappropriately full. I chose eucharis instead. Its whiteness matched the camellias and its long stem provided height

without bulk. Tall angular oil bottles acted as vases, being wide enough at the base to support the flowers' one-sided weight and tapered enough to hold a single flower while also giving a high narrow profile—both important considerations when the container is such an integral part of the composition.

I created a single massive arrangement to decorate the drinks reception area. No single flower could make this impact so I chose to use huge branches of whitebeam, their tiny emerging leaves like butterflies on the bare brown boughs. Such a large, freestanding arrangement had to be balanced and secure, so it was set in a water-filled, white concrete pot, with bricks holding the branches in place. The tallest branches were also wired to overhead beams. Another option would be to use a young growing tree which could be planted after the event.

"Elegance is refusal."

Diana Vreeland

ABOVE Floral art for an art gallery: a wooden picture frame is completely filled with flower heads to decorate a gallery wall. The windowsills are lined with lime-green tolmiea plants in contrasting blue-painted pots, echoing the color of the chairs, and similar painted pots on the tables contain helxines, surrounding a central arrangement of ranunculus.

RIGHT The bride's tied posy: tightly packed apricot ranunculus contrast with lime guelder rose (*Viburnum opulus*).

OPPOSITE The bridesmaid's bouquet is a stronger version of the bride's, using ranunculus in tones ranging from tangerine through peach, to match her vibrant citrus silk dress.

OVERLEAF LEFT (clockwise from top left) Cut ranunculus arranged in a mound with four helxine sentinels makes a pretty table decoration; the blossom of *Malus* 'Lemoinei'; warm pink ranunculus with green *Helleborus foetidus* on another table, again with the accompanying helxines; the yellow bells of crown imperials (*Fritillaria imperialis*).

OVERLEAF RIGHT A pair of "pictures" on the wall–of *Narcissus* 'Cheerfulness' and yellow tulip heads—offsets the exuberance of a mixed arrangement on the bar. The latter comprises burgundy crabapple blossom, guelder rose, striped tulips, crown imperials, trails of scented genista, and young larch with its lime-green leaves just emerging.

In vivid contrast

to the restraint of the previous pages,

an art-gallery restaurant is decorated

here with a painter's palette of colors

using mixed ranunculus and other

bright spring flowers.

This wedding was to be celebrated in a restaurant as modern as the gallery of the previous pages, but it presented a very different challenge, in that ceilings were lower and the room was less well lit. Yet again, the bare walls provided my inspiration: when I discovered that no paintings would be on display at the time of the wedding, I decided to make flower pictures to fill the gaps.

I constructed wooden frames on a base of plain fiberboard sheet, and covered these with a single layer of chicken wire, stapling it into place. The flowers were given a long preparatory drink to ensure that they lasted the night, and then the short stems were woven through with damp moss to create a wash of color. The flowers were tightly packed and able to draw moisture from the moss so they did not deteriorate visibly during the party.

Symmetrically positioned pots (inexpensive terracotta, painted blue) were used to decorate the tables. In varying sizes and proportions, they were filled with either strongly toned ranunculus or mounds of helxines to fill the room with bright color. An exuberant arrangement combined all the colors at the entrance bar. Additional smaller pots could hold night-lights for an evening dinner.

You could fill a frame with colorful dahlias for a late summer version, or with metallic hydrangea heads for a subtler fall variation, complemented by vines and grapes in pewter pots on the tables.

THE COMBINATION OF a clever designer and a bride with a strongly developed personal taste occasionally results in a truly unique wedding dress. A perfect example of such collaboration is shown here. This is, first and foremost, a beautiful dress but that, of course, is not what makes it unique. While its exquisitely delicate, soft green silk is certainly one contributing factor, I believe its most wonderful quality is that it is unusual and yet still manages to look like a wedding gown— a difficult feat. Sometimes, of course, simply aiming to create something that is completely untypical can produce equally glorious results, but this is a rarer and more subtle achievement.

The challenge for the florist is to interpret successfully this blend of tradition and innovation in the wedding flowers. On this occasion, the fact that almost every other color would have looked beautiful with this shade of green made my task particularly difficult. Mixed garden roses would have been sublime; trails of sweet peas in pastel sherbet shades would have been enchantingly pretty; and armfuls of bluebells would have been elegant and simple. However, none of these options seemed quite unusual enough to do justice to the dress. Eventually I realized that if people only remembered

LEFT Bridal "flowers" of dappled green and glaucous foliage perfectly complement the beautiful pale celadon dress. A large green glass vase of wild carrot (*Daucus carota*) stands to one side.
OPPOSITE A verdant silvery green garland, with flowering pink jasmine (*Jasminum officinale*) trailing over whitecurrants in a glass comport.

The Color Green

A subtly alternative dress in a cool classical setting is enhanced with striking foliage-dominated decorations. A generous mixture of frosty, silvered greens, with a hint of flower and berry, creates this calm and harmonious scheme.

one thing about this particular wedding it would be its "greenness," and that, in fact, I did not need to decide which other color would make it special—I simply needed to use more of the same!

My next task was to decide which shades of green to use. I found that darker greens looked dull next to the dress, and opted instead for a mixture of silvery, smoky greens, such as that of helichrysum, with grayish hostas and the cleaner, white-edged greens of the oakleaved geranium. With "all-foliage" arrangements, a very generous hand is required. The use of large quantities of different ingredients ensures that the sense of texture is not lost, and that the result does not look miserly and bereft of flowers. I designed a wired bouquet here so that the end product would be light both in appearance and weight. This allows one to create a more sprawling shape while avoiding unwelcome comparisons with a shrubbery.

The headdress was the next consideration. A pale green veil might have given the bride a very odd complexion, while a hat of the same fabric would have reduced the bridal image, giving it slightly too theatrical a bias. I designed this rather unusual headdress to compensate for both! From the front it looks like a leafy pillbox hat, which enhances the slightly retrospective design of the dress. It is from the back, however, that its full veil-like glory is revealed and best displayed, with its trailing cascade of helichrysum—echoing the shape of the bouquet—creating a romantic effect without detracting from the subtlety of the dress.

It is a good idea with a trailing foliage headdress (which is likely to be worn for several hours) to experiment beforehand to ensure that the foliage you have chosen does not wilt too quickly. Sometimes if you carefully nip out the soft growing-tip you will gain an extra hour or two of pristine appearance.

The bridesmaids were attired in plain ivory dresses, but their flowers continued the green theme. The simple headdresses were made only of geranium leaves and were worn high on the head, a small braid of hair providing a secure base upon which to fix them. A few trails of pinkish-white jasmine in their bouquets lent the merest hint of flowers and served to soften the rather "grown-up" sophistication of unadulterated greenery.

The jasmine flower also played a part in the table decorations. Inspired by the bride's slightly whimsical headdress, I made romantically intricate arrangements: luxuriant garlands of luminous frosty green foliage surrounded a pile of glistening whitecurrants on rented green glass comports, with jasmine tumbling over the whole decoration to soften the formality of the design.

Large-scale, voluptuously floral arrangements would have seemed out of place both with these bridal flowers and their pale and classical surroundings. Instead, I arranged long slender stems of wild carrot in bulbous green glass vases on the floor, to continue the carefully considered lightness and refinement of the whole theme.

LEFT The bridal bouquet is a liberal cascade of silvery *Helichrysum petiolare*, fluffy lambs' ears (*Stachys byzantina*), scented variegated geranium, hosta leaves (*Hosta sieboldiana*), fluffy clematis seed heads (*Clematis alpina*), and, as a token gesture toward flowers, a few greenish-purple flower heads of *Nectaroscordum siculum*, a beautiful summer-flowering bulb.

ABOVE The matching headdress—whose shape reflects that of the bouquet—is basically a high band of scented geranium leaves with sprays of the smoky green helichrysum trailing down and entwined with the bride's hair.

OPPOSITE One of the bridesmaids holds a small posy of deliciously scented geranium leaves and pink jasmine, tied with a pale green silk ribbon to match the bride's dress. Her headdress is based on the bride's in concept and form, and resembles its basic structure, but with the flamboyant trailing helichrysum omitted in order to retain a simple charm.

JUST AS THE PAST can inspire an apparently infinite variety of wedding styles, so too can the traditions and tastes of other cultures. The western world has always been fascinated by the East and there is still much to be learned—esthetically and metaphysically. Designers of wedding dresses, who have long looked to western historical costume for inspiration, are now almost imperceptibly—introducing eastern influences into their contemporary collections.

If you attempt to produce too accurate a copy of a culturally specific style, you will almost inevitably encounter the same problems as you would do if you tried to design a strictly authentic historical theme. Given the unavailability of the real ingredients and lack of particular skills, you might well end up with an unflattering caricature. Accuracy is perhaps more of a necessity for an intercultural marriage but, even then, a style which is a fusion of both traditions will produce a more diplomatic and complementary result.

This dress is an authentic Indian wedding costume made of intense red silk, overlaid with golden organza and heavily embroidered in shades of gold and silver. Its shimmering nebulous color is both its chief glory and the florist's greatest problem, for no single color could match

LEFT Dramatic decorations for a plain setting: huge gilded urns on tall stands are filled to overflowing with scarlet peonies, intensely colored trailing bougainvillea, *Rosa* 'Albertine' and lilies (*Lilium* 'Orlando').
OPPOSITE Golden pots of miniature red roses underplanted with grass form an arching centerpiece for the table, with a peony at each place.

East-West

An eclectic mixture of eastern influences gives this wedding a vibrantly intense palette. Inspired by the rich tones of India, it is tempered by the restraint of plain, angular containers more in the mood of Japan or China; the result is style without pastiche.

ABOVE AND RIGHT The bride's flowers were inspired by the traditional eastern lei—a thick necklace of flowers—here adapted to fall over one shoulder to emphasize the asymmetrical style of the bride's shawl. The headdress sweeps elegantly around the opposite side of her head, creating the illusion that it is part of the same floral garland sensually spiralling around her body. It is made by binding flower heads on to a piece of string, using the peach-colored rose 'Doris-Rykin', with pelargoniums in shades of pink and maroon, fuchsias combining reds and pinks, and solidly colored apricot, red, and coral kalanchoe flowers. These combined elements reflect and reinforce the singing colors and iridescence of the bride's richly embroidered gown.

RIGHT Flowers for the dining tables at a candlelit evening reception. The same vibrant colors and flowers have been arranged more softly and naturally in Indian iron-and-blown-glass pots set upon pink silk tablecloths. This is altogether a gentler, less stylized look than the one shown on previous pages, although little pots of kalanchoe flower heads are scattered across the tables to link these decorations with the more intense style of the bridal flowers.

it exactly: peach-colored roses would have looked exquisite in some lights, while in others the harsh red of kalanchoes might have seemed perfect. Instead, the layers of color that created the dress needed to be balanced by similar layers in the flowers, so I mixed varieties and colors in a closely packed, undiluted way. This would have produced a heavy-looking bouquet, but it was absolutely right for the lei style of decoration used here. A lei is traditionally made on string so that it has movement—crucial for both comfort and appearance. Here, I designed it to be worn over one shoulder, echoing the line of the shawl. The headdress that completed the bride's floral decoration also emphasizes this asymmetry.

Large-scale "oriental" decorations proved to be another problem. Tree branches, which would have been suitably linear, would not be colorful enough, yet a western-style arrangement would have been inappropriate, even if it had contained the correct combination of colors. Instead, I used whole bougainvillea plants as the skeleton of a very "unwestern" arrangement, which tumbled from tall wooden urns on stands. These were arranged with other cut flowers (in raised buckets of water) for scent and more color. I sprayed the containers with three shades of metallic gold over black, giving them a burnished effect to echo the dress.

I used small, similarly shaped containers on the tables, in which I placed growing rose plants with some of their gnarled roots exposed, creating a "bonsai" effect. A contrasting sash of rich velvet was laid across the table, to resemble a Japanese obi, and waterlily-like peonies were positioned—as if floating—at each place. The cumulative effect of these elements, amid the abundant richness and intensity of the east Indian decorations, created an oasis of calm serenity.

The mingling scents

of tuberoses and Madonna lilies

create an intoxicating atmosphere

reminiscent of heady eastern aromas,

while their cool, waxy whiteness gives

a simple contemporary edge to this

beautiful wedding scheme.

The lively colors and authentically ethnic textures of the eastern world have long been hugely influential in the West. In recent years, however, it has been the spirituality of these peoples and their meditative outlook on life that have become all-pervasive, determining our move toward calmer visual environments and a more minimalist approach to design at all levels. Whereas the vibrant colors of a traditional eastern dress seemed to need a sumptuous setting, with the flowers required to transform the simple modern venue, here the bride's beaded dress sat well in the starkness of the room, so the role of the flowers was simply to enhance the theme.

With their ancient eastern origins, long-stemmed lilies arranged in a plain urn gave an appropriately exotic air to the decorations. Moreover, their heady fragrance, combined with that of the tuberoses which formed a wreath for the bride's hair, left the air heavily perfumed like an incense-filled eastern palace. I did not think the bride needed other flowers, but a single lily stem, elegantly and artlessly held, could be a striking touch.

Inspired by the extraordinarily skillful florists of India, who create whole pergolas from strings of flowers for weddings, I made some more modest floral earrings, using a needle and thread, and single flower heads.

ABOVE In calm contrast to the vibrant scheme of the previous pages, a large old oil jar is packed with waving stems of the intoxicatingly scented Madonna lily (*Lilium candidum*) to provide a cool and timelessly stylish large-scale arrangement which is perfectly in keeping with the plain, but pungently fragrant, scheme chosen for the bridal flowers.

ABOVE LEFT AND ABOVE The waxy whiteness of the Madonna lily is echoed in the equally heady perfume of the tuberose. Individual flowers are threaded on to wire to produce this simple headdress—an echo of the row of pearls edging the bridal gown.
LEFT The same flower-threading technique could be used rather more adventurously to produce exquisitely complex "jewelry" such as flower necklaces or bracelets, or even earrings like those shown here which comprise a tuberose flower and the individual florets from a white sweet William (*Dianthus barbatus*) flower head.

FLORISTS DESIGNING FLOWERS for country weddings sometimes suffer inexplicable delusions of grandeur. Perhaps it is the effect of all that open space, or maybe it is a subconscious sense of obligation to prove one's talents and show that the money has indeed been well spent—and all hedgerows left intact. To my eye the results can sometimes appear overwhelmingly artificial and look out-of-place. It is one thing to decorate a marquee in a country garden for a cleverly themed evening party but quite another to take guests through wild-flower meadows between a church and a marquee—and to have decorated both with expensive out-of-season lilies and carnations. Of course, the bride and her choice of style for the day should set an appropriate look, and not every bride wants pretty country-style flowers and clothes simply because of the location. However, there are inspiring alternatives, and this is one of them. Its light-hearted, fresh, and unpretentious approach seems to me perfectly suited to this relaxed summer country setting, without sacrificing any sense of style.

As ever, the bride's dress was the main original inspiration for the whole scheme. In itself it is quite alternative—being short and plain—but the delicate

LEFT Simple and unaffected: comfortable clothing and country flowers offer a stylish alternative to the traditional white wedding.
OPPOSITE Marguerites, the mainstay of all these wedding decorations, are arranged in a galvanized metal pan as if growing through long grass, to make a quirky outdoor table treatment.

The Power of Flower

Casual, comfortable, and with a definite sense of humor, this fresh and relaxed approach to country wedding flowers, taking simple daisies as its theme, is totally unpretentious but certainly demonstrates a thing or two about real style!

"Daisy, Daisy,

Give me your answer do,

I'm half crazy,

All for the love of you."

Song from the 1890s

ABOVE AND RIGHT In keeping with the relaxed mood of the day, the bridesmaids carry bunches of marguerites and marigolds (calendula), tied simply and artlessly with bright gingham ribbon. Their headdresses are bands of daisies with some of the flowers left on longer stems to create a wilder "unkempt" look, to complement their bouquets. The hair itself is twisted back over the bands to hold them in place, and secured with two clips–decorated once again with a few daisy heads.

scattering of embroidered daisies gives it a sweet and special quality which is thoroughly "bridal." Unusually, given that it was my intention to create an alternative look, I decided to give the bride a veil. Somehow it seemed to match the retrospective feeling of the dress, which could almost come from a late 1960s fashion show. Short and full, the veil also has that look of an *ingénue* which seemed to suit the bride perfectly. Again, to be different, and to link it with the dress, I attached a shower of daisy heads all over the tulle, using a hot glue-gun. A band covered in daisy heads held it in place.

A simple posy of daisies would have made the perfect bridal bouquet and indeed, given a more classical style of long dress, with similar embroidery, this would have been my first choice. However, in this case I wanted to make a bouquet that would be slightly more sophisticated—to give the bride impact—and witty too, as that seemed to suit the mood that was developing.

The result was this tied circular posy. Its style was loosely based on traditional Victorian posies, with concentric rings of flowers. This quaint idea suited the country setting but there was a twist to it: by using white flowers on the outside rings and bright yellow in the center, I had created what was, to all intents and purposes, a single, large daisy head from the combination of flowers. Although this was a subtle pun, visually, the bouquet was strong, and bold enough to be independent of the daisy embroidery of the dress in a way that a simpler bouquet might not have been. A loose bow of gingham ribbon added a casual finishing touch.

Flowers for the bridesmaids repeated the daisy theme and stood out perfectly against their fresh yellow cotton dresses. They carried rustic bunches of marguerites and marigolds (calendula) gathered together in the most casual way, in contrast to the bride's more sophisticated posy. The content and the gingham ribbon were the only visual links. Their hair too was decorated with daisy bands, the flower heads wired and arranged in such a way as to give the illusion that they had simply been pushed into the hair. Daisies are the perfect choice for

ABOVE Embroidered with daisies, the bridal dress sets the theme for the day. The bride's posy-shaped bouquet is a careful blend of the natural and the stylized: bands of the tiny daisy-flowered feverfew (*Chrysanthemum parthenium*) and larger marguerites surround a central core of bright marigolds (*calendula*). The idea is to create a cross between an old-fashioned Victorian posy and a visual pun on the daisy theme. Again it is finished with a sash of simple gingham ribbon.

OPPOSITE The wedding cake floats on a cloud of feverfew, its tiers circled with orderly rows of larger daisy heads with a cheerful bunch waving from the top. **RIGHT** Bridal flowers with a difference: these daisy-framed sunglasses were made by attaching flower heads to an inexpensive pair of white plastic sunglasses, using a hot glue-gun. They last perfectly well after this treatment and make a witty alternative to the proverbial rose-tinted spectacles!

young bridesmaids. Their open faces have always been linked with youth and, in the language of flowers, they are symbolic of innocent times and companionship.

Decorations for the luncheon tables dotted across the lawn were in keeping with the unpretentious mood: galvanized pans appeared to have been filled with blocks of daisy-strewn turf. It was, of course, a simple illusion. Nevertheless, it looked appropriate and stylish in its outdoor—albeit daisy-free—setting. Placing one flower on every gingham-tied napkin is the sort of detail that really establishes a theme at a wedding, giving the impression that everything about the day has been organized with great care and thought.

The cake was decorated with bands of flower heads similar to, but in a more orderly version of, the children's headdresses. These and the jaunty bunch on the top were simply pushed into the soft icing wherever they were required to be. Of course, if you are worried about damaging the cake, a similar effect could be achieved by making garlands of daisies on wires which would fit exactly around each tier.

And finally—for the very alternative bride, or as a cute accessory for her to wear as she leaves for the honeymoon—pert daisy sunglasses like these would cause a sensation in most country circles! Whoever told Daisy that it would not be a stylish marriage?

CONTEMPORARY BRIDES are increasingly inclined to choose dresses that make them feel comfortable on their special day—especially more "mature" brides or those marrying for the second (or subsequent) time. Happily, today there are no rules and the modern bride can be influenced by fashion rather than tradition.

This dress, made of rich chocolate-brown brocade in an exquisitely simple style, is undeniably special and suitable for any big occasion. Most importantly, however, it will have a longer life than most wedding dresses!

From the flower point of view there are two ways to approach this type of bridal style. One can reinterpret traditional concepts to suit the unusual color and simple tailoring, or one can design something as unusual and individual as the dress itself. The latter approach requires a bride confident enough both to carry off something out of the ordinary, and to trust her florist to succeed in producing a suitably quirky look.

The happiest results derive from a lot of discussion, flexibility and instinct. Given the "Jackie O" style of the dress, my immediate instinct here was to abandon traditional hair decorations and posies in favor of the pill-box hat creation that was the starting point of the whole look. A headdress like this must not be too smart;

LEFT In deference to tradition this individual bride wears flowers—but in the form of a witty hat and bag made of oakleaves and fall fruits.
OPPOSITE Traditionally, the oakleaf symbolizes love's endurance, and strength. This jaunty hat, made of oakleaves and berries, combines the ancient sentiment with a thoroughly contemporary sense of style.

Café Society

The bridal sensation here is achieved with simple bravado rather than acres of white silk. A neatly tailored brocade dress is given rather individual accessories in this novel autumnal interpretation of traditional wedding flowers.

ABOVE (clockwise from top left)
The bridegroom for such a stylish bride deserves more than just a decorative waistcoat. While still complementing the bride's "flowers," these three buttonhole ideas have a hint of rebellion. A miniature pineapple—the ancient symbol of friendship and welcome so often carved atop gateposts—with a few tradescantia leaves and alder cones; a glistening cluster of blackberries, with rosehips and oakleaves echoing the bride; and a single perky little crabapple, a stem of dusky sloeberries, and a few bronze oakleaves to match the bride's accessories. The components of all three are first wired and then bound together into a suitable size and shape.

OPPOSITE The bridal purse! Hypericum berries and crabapples offer texture and interest among the preserved oakleaves that cover the foam shape, with a slightly more quirky effect than the plainer leaf decoration of the hat. They were all attached straight on to the dry foam using a hot glue-gun.

> *"Why not be oneself? That is the whole secret of a successful appearance. If one is a greyhound, why try to look like a Pekingese?"*

Dame Edith Sitwell

it must come across as a hat rather than as a lump of flowers. I decided to keep it very plain—rather tailored and shapely like the dress. I sewed glycerined oakleaves (available from dried-flower suppliers) in a regular overlapping pattern on to a purchased fabric hat shape. Using preserved leaves means that an anxious bride can approve the finished item before the big day. A trim of fresh flowers or, as here, a few bright glistening berries, can be added at the last minute.

The shape of the leafy purse was copied from a fashion magazine. Using a hot glue-gun, leaves were attached over the whole surface of a form cut from dry florist's foam and trimmed to preserve the shape. The bag was then generously sprinkled with berries and crabapples, creating a colorful and textured finish to stand out against the darker background of the dress. Finally, a suitable twig was carefully bent and glued firmly to the foam as a handle.

Obviously, neither hat nor purse should be attempted by the nervous bride on the morning of the wedding; they are the products of a skilled florist's labor.

Any bride who chooses such a subtle color palette and individual style for her wedding would be unwise to ruin the picture by hanging flowers on every surface. The look is contemporary and, for all its daring, quite understated—hardly the choice for a huge gathering where its subtlety would be lost in the crowd. Other decorations should be minimal, but equally stylish and considered in their attention to detail: a wedding cake of cream chocolate could be sprinkled with the tiniest oakleaves—each held on by a single berry—or have a fountain of blackberries in the center. Oakleaves could be scattered on linen tablecloths, with floating candles and berries decorating central glass bowls of water. If flowers were felt to be lacking, an alternative would be roses such as 'Vicci Brown' with its combination of terracotta and beige, or 'Leonidis' which is a copper-tan color.

It would be difficult to repeat this look in other seasons. A purse or hat made entirely of rose heads is almost too pretty to be perceived as part of a costume. Better, I think, to keep to a plain basis of preserved leaves with a few, well-chosen flowers as a finishing detail.

Stylishly simple:

a pared-down elegance pervades this casual approach to the same unusual dress. Color is still the guiding light— but used in a less stylized way, without sacrificing impact.

Not every bride would feel comfortable with the novelty of the ideas on the previous few pages. Perhaps a particularly understated dress has been chosen not to proclaim individuality but to bring a subtle dignity to a small celebration—a second marriage, for example.

Whatever the case, it would be a shame for the flowers to disturb the simplicity or to make the wearer feel self-conscious. Here, while returning to the more traditional ideas of both bouquet and flowers, I avoided the almost ubiquitous circular posy in favor of this more sweeping style, designing a rich burgundy, chocolate, and purple tied bouquet using wickedly sybaritic calla lilies, combined with grape leaves and grapes. With the flower heads packed together in this controlled, rather formal way, the result is surprisingly unaffected, and the perfect accessory for this dress— unusual, refined, and classically simple. A similarly unpretentious headdress would be difficult to design, but a simple band of grape leaves or a hat trimmed with leaves and callas could complete the picture.

A more natural style of flower-arranging provides the opportunity for creating larger-scale displays like this one. In this classical setting the choice of container is, as ever, a good starting point. Rather than the more obvious urn, I chose this old oil jar—combining age and elegant proportions with novelty and a hint of exotic

climes. Its height and weight are further advantages and allow the use of heavy branches covered in crabapples, without balance becoming a problem. It also allows this beautifully disarrayed style of arranging in which the stems are held in place by the jar's narrow neck.

In summer this look could be achieved with a bouquet of unusual roses: the English roses 'Cymbeline' or 'Charles Rennie Mackintosh', for example, teamed with the bronzed leaves of *Heuchera* 'Palace Purple'. A simple urn, filled with young copper beech branches, would look glorious with sunlight filtering through the topaz leaves.

OPPOSITE This tied bouquet of waxy purple calla lilies, closely packed together with a few chocolate-brown grape leaves and a stem or two of unripened grapes, offers a less stylized but equally stylish approach. Ripe grapes could very easily stain the dress and should be avoided!
ABOVE A relaxed, disarrayed arrangement of crabapple stems, blackberries, and a trio of silvery cardoon leaves (*Cynara cardunculus*) in a beautiful old stone oil jar gives a sense of scale without formality.

VULGAR, CAMP, OUTRAGEOUS—this color scheme is not for the wilting violet! This magnificent dress has classical elements, but color is not one of them. It is a lively blend of orange-red silk with a flowing pink organza overdress, and is not overawed by the opulent and dramatic setting. My challenge was to produce flowers that could stand up to these colors and create an equally individual ambience. For the bridal bouquet I chose Icelandic poppies, their flimsy, floating petals perfectly matching the delicate overdress and the crabapples adding a touch of gaiety and fall fruitfulness. I wanted my flowers to blend with the unique dress color rather than competing with it, as a contrasting stronger color might have done, because the effect is altogether richer and more flattering.

The bride's high upswept hairstyle is outlined with a crescent of crabapples, nerines, and poppies, each individually wired to keep weight to a minimum, and so prevent the hair being dragged down. Anything heavy would also jar with the lightness of the bridal gown.

As a floral decorator, my task was to marry this dress to its rich surroundings. Scale was a paramount consideration, so I rented several huge gilt gothic candelabra from a theatrical prop company to create an avenue along which the bride would make her dramatic entrance. These were

LEFT An avenue of gilt candelabra garlanded with burgundy amaryllis flowers, half-pomegranates, and swathes of red silk creates intense background coloring for an equally vibrant bridal gown.
OPPOSITE The bouquet comprises Icelandic poppies in vermilion, orange, and fuchsia pink, with small branches of crabapples.

Gothic Baroque

The antithesis of traditional wedding flowers, this cacophony of vibrant color—a glorious autumnal mixture of poppies, pomegranates, amaryllis, and crabapples—creates a magnificent contrast to the startling dress.

"Vulgarity is a very important ingredient in life. I'm a great believer in vulgarity—if it's got vitality."

Diana Vreeland

decorated with amaryllis flowers and pomegranates, wired and bound on to a rope. Greenery is usually used to hide gaps and fill out the arrangement but, rather than dilute these colors with green, I draped inexpensive red lining silk around the garlands to fall in swathes over the floor.

I rented props for other decorations, too: a mound of pomegranates and the hairy burgundy pods of hibiscus flower buds were piled on a gilt platter for a simple-yet-opulent table decoration. Scaled-down versions of the large candelabra could have been used instead. For the buffet tables I rented old copper and bronze urns and firmly fixed a pole about 4 feet high into each. These were then covered with wet florist's foam held together with chicken wire and finished with moss. Formal spirals of flowers and fruits were added to make baroque pillars, each topped with a pineapple. This effect echoes the draped candelabra and the bride's swirling hair decoration, creating a subtly unified look.

Another garland was designed to swirl down the plain white wedding cake. Bound on to garden twine, it was strong but flexible, and could be made in advance, then stored in damp tissue paper until required.

Finally, the bridegroom's poppy buttonhole provides the sort of finishing detail which epitomizes any well-thought-out scheme. It would be all too easy to overlook this, but simply using a traditional white rose would greatly diminish the overall effect.

OPPOSITE (clockwise from top left)
A swirl of poppies, crabapples, and nerines in the bride's upswept hair; a gilt platter of pomegranates and hibiscus buds decorates a small table; the bridegroom has a quirky buttonhole of a single papery, wired Icelandic poppy; the simple cake, decorated with a swag of poppies, nerines, crabapples, and anemones in clashing shades of pink and topped with a huge amaryllis flower.
ABOVE A large copper urn holds a statuesque arrangement for the buffet table: spirals of pomegranates, crabapples, amaryllis, and anemones topped with a single pink pineapple fringed with nerines.

Retro-chic

is explored in this alternative approach to the same vibrant wedding dress. The look here is fashionable rather than theatrical, producing a subtle style, suitable for a smaller wedding.

A less flamboyant but equally lively look was the aim here. With a stylized bouquet of orange and bright pink tulips and a simple bow decorated with nerines, the dress is treated as a contemporary fashion statement rather than a theatrical costume, as on the previous pages. Indeed, the whole look has been pared down, making it suitable for a more intimate wedding where large-scale decorations are less crucial to the event.

The shape of the bride's bouquet is an elegant interpretation of the more downward-pointing bouquets of the 1960s and early '70s, while avoiding the tightly packed circle of flowers so common today. It is also a shape that nestles comfortably in the hand. The tulips were individually wired and an outline of the final shape was made with a few blooms. In this way, the best overall size and proportions could be decided before the solid center was filled in. I try to maintain some sense of delicacy in these solid flower bouquets by keeping the size small, otherwise the effect can be very unwieldy.

For the bride's long bouffant hair I made a simple flat bow of wired ribbon in shot silk and decorated it with a few individually wired nerine flowers and buds. The bow is designed to sit jauntily on the back of the head without any apparent role in securing the hair. This is a rare exception to the rule—I generally find headdresses more successful when they appear to play a vital part in maintaining a hairstyle.

Bowls of tulip heads in the same mixed colors could decorate the tables, or perhaps each table could be restricted to one shade. Bigger decorations would be more of a challenge if one wanted to maintain a similar intensity of color. Large gilded urns of vivid pink cherry blossom would work well with the tulip decorations if the seasonal weather were to permit such a combination, and mixing different types of blossom would produce an even stronger, more colorful effect.

To reproduce a similar result in the summer months, the obvious flowers for this sort of bouquet would be rosebuds, while bunches of vivid roses would produce equally dramatic—though more costly—decorative effects in the ornamentation of the rooms. An organized and thrifty bride might plan well in advance and grow vibrant shades of petunias, geraniums, and other annuals to use—either cut or growing—for a summer wedding that required strident color schemes.

OPPOSITE AND RIGHT A wired bridal bouquet in retrospective vein: a 1960s-inspired lip-shaped bouquet of various orange and pink tulips, formally clustered in a solid mass of color that is undiluted by greenery of any kind.

Planning your wedding flowers

When to start

If the overall esthetics of the wedding day are important to you, the earlier in the planning process the flowers are considered, the better. These are widely acknowledged to be the unifying, finishing touch and, when particularly successful, are the one aspect of the day that will be long-remembered. They are worth getting right. It may seem excessively biased to suggest that flowers are an ideal starting point, but nature certainly has more experience than most brides when it comes to choosing colors. The shades of spring flowers suit spring light, for instance, and the vibrancy of fall berries warms a dismal fall evening. At the very least, considering the season and its floral highlights at an early stage will avoid a headache for your florist later on!

Choosing a floral decorator

There can be no finer recommendation than word of mouth—especially if you have already seen the florist's work. Looking at decorators' portfolios can be useful, but these only show what he or she has already done—not what is possible. They can also prompt you to fix upon an idea too soon—often with little relevance to current circumstances—which could result in a remix of themes and color schemes from other weddings rather than the development of an appropriate individual design. It is therefore better to look at portfolios once your initial thoughts have been discussed. Instinct is also important. You and the florist need to work well together to achieve the best results on the day, and the design process should always be a collaborative effort.

Gathering ideas

I like to look at the chosen dress when I need a catalyst for initial floral ideas. As I have said, it is also best if the color scheme is chosen with the season in mind. With any luck, it will also suit the venue—but this is not always so!

I made inspirational pinboards for the twenty floral schemes in this book. These are far more useful, I believe, than having several files full of completely diverse components. Each pinboard was essentially made up of magazine photographs, bits of fabric, and any paint swatches that seemed to suit the scheme—seldom with any reference to actual flowers. Postcards of paintings dating from the same period as the venue or the style of the bridal dress also supplied valuable information about jewelry and colors. All these elements combined to create a complete rather than a diffused "look." Once a theme is established, actually choosing and arranging the flowers is quite easy, and this is where the experienced florist comes into his or her own.

To do or not to do?

It is obviously with some degree of self-interest that I would recommend using a professional florist or floral decorator for your big day. I might qualify this by saying that a wedding can be one of the most stressful and angst-ridden occasions of your life, and years of personal experience has certainly taught me that, however well organized, the days immediately leading up to a wedding are frantically busy. This is, of course, when one would need to organize the flowers, and trying to arrange them in the midst of a trauma is not to be recommended!

On the day itself, most brides manage at least some semblance of calm—if an entourage of hairdressers and make-up artists can be considered calming—and to give up even this small token luxury to arrange last-minute flowers seems to me to be faintly masochistic. For those undeterred, however, I offer some useful guidelines opposite. As final thoughts on the subject, might I suggest that, if you are organizing your own flowers, you should never underestimate the power of simplicity; I would also recommend avoiding wired items such as headdresses—or leaving them to the experts.

Arranging your own flowers

Working out quantities

Flower-arranging for large events is like working out an inspired recipe and cooking it for several people—the inspiration is the hard part. Thereafter, limited mathematical skills and energy are all that are needed to reproduce the recipe several times over. It is best—even for the smallest wedding—to work everything out on paper. Moreover, if you are inexperienced, you might like to give yourself a trial run, by designing one table centerpiece a few weeks before the event. It is at this stage that you can adjust its contents; the exercise will also be useful for estimating the quantities of the flowers you need to order. Multiply each of the contents by the number of repeats you have planned and this will give you a shopping list for your trip to the flower store.

Timing the work

Approach this like a recipe, too. Preparation can take place up to several days in advance—containers painted, flowers conditioned—and you can pace this to suit your other commitments. The actual arranging time is often more problematic because it cannot be paced in the same way. Flowers do not live forever and the location may only be available a few hours before the wedding. Take, for example, a single table centerpiece. It may take half an hour to create this one arrangement. Multiply this by twenty tables and you have ten hours' work, and this does not take into account the time it takes to set up tables and to clear the debris when you have finished! Alternatively, you could employ five people to work for two hours. Calculate all these timings and how many people you will need well in advance—certainly while you still have time to call in a professional florist in a crisis!

Buying the flowers

I cannot really give advice about where you should buy your flowers. A wholesale market will obviously be less expensive, but a store may be able to offer some much-needed practical tips, or to lend buckets to keep flowers cool. It is usually better to buy your flowers over a period of several days so that some flower buds have time to open. This very necessary floral skill can only be acquired through experience—no one wants hundreds of unopened amaryllis the day before the wedding! Choosing the right flowers can also avoid this problem: sweet peas, for example, in full perfection, can be bought as close to the day as possible. Quality counts at this stage more than anything else.

Conditioning flowers

All flowers benefit from being correctly handled before they are arranged. There is simply no room here to give a comprehensive list of treatments, but there are many books to which you can turn for this information. If in doubt, however, simply re-cut each stem and place the flowers in cold water in a cool place for at least a day before you arrange them. Again, this task may take several hours if you have a lot of flowers.

Keeping to schedule

The most difficult part! When you devise your schedule, while aiming to finish several hours early, over-estimate the time every procedure will take, for no bride wants to have just three minutes to wash, dress, and remove green stains. Remember that exhaustion and excitement are not conducive to hard work or good personnel management. Decide on your priorities and tackle them first so that nothing that really matters to you falls victim to panic.

Finishing touches

Ultimately, it is these that both define a professional edge and often cause the most stress. Remember that only you know the extent of your proposed design and thus it is probably only you who will notice if anything is omitted. Do not fuss unnecessarily over the angle of the bows on 400 napkins; the larger the function, the less the intricate details will be noticed!

Acknowledgments

Brides' dresses

Each of the wonderful dresses photographed in this book was an essential element in the overall look of individual stories and many were also the initial inspiration behind the choice of flowers. We would like to thank the following designers for lending us their creations:

Helen Arnold (cape p 92); Alison Blake (pp 68–71, 78–85); Bridal Rogue Gallery (pp 58–9); Neil Cunningham (front cover, pp 28–31, 60–7, 106–7, 132–7); Sharon Hoey (pp 128–31, 48–51); Gillian Leavy (pp 42–5); Phillipa Lepley (pp 12–17, 74–5, 92–7, 98–9); Deborah Milner (pp 110–13); Jenny Packham (pp 102–5); Rivaaz (pp 114–17, 118–19); Soie Meme (pp 46–7); Tomasz Starzewski (pp 18–19, 32–5, 126–31); Rebecca Street (pp 20–3, 24–7, 120–5); Ritva Westenius (pp 54–7); Basia Zarzycka (pp 72–3);

Special thanks to Emily Louden and Candida Denniston for lending us their own wedding dresses to photograph.

Bridesmaids' dresses

Bridal Rogue Gallery (pp 39, 55–6, 60–5); Neil Cunningham (pp 30, 71, 107); Freddie Boy Children's Wear (p 17); Pretty Mades (pp 35, 77); Soie Meme (p 47); Rebecca Street (p 20)

Menswear and Accessories

Moss Bros; Gabriella Lingenza; Anya Hindmarch; Butler & Wilson; Ernest Jones; Emma Hope

Venues

The beautiful settings were an equal pleasure and inspiration. We would like to offer our warmest thanks to those concerned for their help and co-operation in the following locations:

The Banqueting House, London (pp 86–91)
The House of St Barnabas in Soho, London (pp 12–19)
Carshalton Water Tower (pp 34–41) ,
By kind permission of the Daughters of the Cross,
The Delfina Studio Cafe (pp 102–9)
Fourth Floor (pp 126–31)
The ICA Galleries (pp 42–7)
The Landmark Hotel (pp 20–7)
Marble Hill House (pp 32–5)
By kind permission of English Heritage,
The Church of St Michael and All Angels (pp 54–9)
The Octagon Room (pp 74–7)
The Orangery (pp 48–51)
Stowe, Landscape Gardens (pp 28–31)
By kind permission of the National Trust
Walpole's House (pp 132–7)
Whitbourne Hall (pp 92–9)

We would also like to thank the following for so kindly allowing us to photograph in their homes or gardens:
Mr and Mrs Dominic Bon de Sousa; Mr and Mrs Henry Wynn; Dr The Rev and Mrs Robin Denniston; The residents of Lloyd Square; Andrew Mortada; Mr and Mrs Eric Wetter de Sanchez.

Wedding cakes

Our thanks to the following shops for lending wedding cakes:
Fileric Cakes (p 62); Suzelle Cakes Limited (pp 70, 124)

China and props

Thanks for the following for lending the essential details that completed each picture:
The Conran Shop; The General Trading Company; Nicholas Haslam; Joanna Wood Limited; Titanus Limited; Clifton Nurseries Limited; Tempus Stet

Bridal party

No thanks could be adequate for these patient souls who endured hours of tweaking without the reward of a real wedding or even a glass of champagne at the end of it all!

Brides

Our gratitude to Karsten Edwards of 'IMM' for providing the beautiful models:
Caroline Berryman; Emma Caesari; Janie Dickens; Georgina French; Joanna Heath; Claire Napier; Christina Nicole; Claire Peckham; Regina Rodriges; Nancy Sorrell; Jane Velerio and Yasmin.

And thanks to the equally beautiful volunteer models:
Sally Jo Caddy; Tessa Clayton; Leigh Robieson-Cleaver; Sue Sharpless and Sara Westley.

Bridesmaids, pageboy and groom

Our thanks to the remaining models in our bridal party:
Eulalie-Rose Bon de Sousa; Shelby Capocci; Holly Dennison; Poppy and Iona Denniston; Peter Dixon; Ailsa Dormon; Rosie, Megan and Sally Evans; Phoebe Fleming; Victoria Hanson; Ella Haynes; Amanda Lerwill; Portland Mitchell; Oliver Watson; Zoe Winlow and Sarah Wright.

And finally, by the kind permission of Mrs Bill Evans—Hamlet the horse.

Author's Acknowledgments

Being commissioned to write a book about wedding flowers is the ultimate indulgence for an opinionated flower person and I cannot thank my publishers enough for entrusting me with such a treasure. They placed me in very capable hands and my greatest thanks must be to the rest of the team whose book it is as much mine.

Jan Baldwin, for perfectly capturing (and often creating) the ambience and moreover being the voice of sense and calm in the storm; Leslie Harrington (ably assisted by Amanda Lerwill) who lived and breathed every page with me and whose masterful arrangement of Jan's pictures makes the book so visually exciting; Kate Bell, always the most patient and diplomatic of editors, who was involved at every stage with ideas and advice; and finally to Suzannah Gough for commissioning it all in the first place.

Like any wedding, each of the twenty stories was a logistical nightmare! A very sincere thank you to those who paved the way; Sylvie Jones (assisted by Portland Mitchell) for synchronizing many disparate elements, finding willing bridesmaids and still managing to produce a baby halfway through the year; Tracey Elson for assisting me on several photography sessions—her superb floral talents, and those of Sharon Melehi and Jo Hughes can be seen in many photographs but they cannot show the humour, support and friendship which I so deeply appreciate in them. My thanks also to the other flower colleagues: Nigel Watts, Cynthia Wood, Samantha Davis and John Pulsome for their encouragement and help with the 'real work'; the hair and make-up artists who interpreted our vague mumbles and gesticulations to such brilliant effect: Evelynne Stoikou, Barbara Braunlich, Firyal Arneil and Margaret Richardson who bravely took us on in Worcestershire.

My thanks also to those who supplied the beautiful flowers: Christine Corson who sent boxes of treasures from her garden to gladden the heart (thank you to Lord and Lady Harmsworth for ferrying them from Devon!); David Austin for heavenly English roses from his nursery; and in Covent Garden: David Gortin at A&F Bacon; Dick at Rimark; Teddy at Page Munro; Dennis at Austins; Alan and Stella at Alagar; Bill and Bobby at Mills; Steve and Adam at Miles and John at Arnott & Mason.

I have been extremely fortunate in the real brides who have commissioned me—the experiences have made this book possible and my heartfelt thanks to them all and to the party planners who have recommended me to many of them: Princess Dora Loewenstein (Dora Loewenstein Associates); Kate and Emma (The Lumsden Twins); Philip, Johnnie and Rowlene (The Admirable Crichton); James (Mustard Catering) and Stevie (Stephen Congdon Party Planning). Lastly my thanks to those special people who don't need to be told what it is for: Michael Goulding (OBE); Elizabeth Barker (MBE); Caroline Feinnes; my ever supportive parents Gerry and Peggy Connolly; and my own personal bride Candida.

Index

Page numbers in *italic* refer to the illustrations

Flowers by season

The following information groups the flowers that I have used (and some that I would like to have used) into the specific seasons in which they were photographed for this book. Several are also available throughout the year. The list is by no means exhaustive, but is intended to provide a simple starting point from which to begin planning your own wedding flowers. It includes those available as growing plants as well as several types of foliage which are particularly beautiful in season.

Spring

Auricula
Bergenia leaves
Blossom (e.g. cultivars of
  Prunus and *Malus*)
Bluebell (*Scilla nutans*)
Broom (*Genista*)
Calla (Arum) lily
  (*Zantedeschia
  aethiopica*)
Camellia
Canterbury bell
  (*Campanula medium*)
Cardoon leaves
  (*Cynara cardunculus*)
Clematis montana
Cowslip (*Primula veris*)
Daffodil
Eucharis
Euphorbia
Forget-me-not (*Myosotis*)
Foxglove (*Digitalis*)
Fritillary
Gardenia
Guelder rose
  (*Viburnum opulus*)
Hellebore
Helxine
Iris
Jasmine
Jonquil
Lilac (*Syringa vulgaris*)
Lily-of-the-valley
  (*Convallaria majalis*)
Mexican orange blossom
  (*Choisya ternata*)
Narcissus
Pansy (*Viola*)
Poppy
Primrose (*Primula vulgaris*)

Ranunculus
Rose (*Rosa banksiae*)
Solomon's seal (*Polygonatum*)
Sorbus (*Sorbus aria*
  'Lutescens' and
  S. cashmiriana)
Spiraea
Tolmiea menziesii
Tulip
Viburnum (*Viburnum* x
  burkwoodii, V. x *bodnantense*
  and *V. fragrans*)

Summer

African marigold (*Tagetes*)
Alchemilla mollis
Aruncus dioicus
Bergenia leaves
Bougainvillea
Bouvardia
Campanula persicifolia
Delphinium
Eucryphia
Feverfew
Fuchsia
Galtonia candicans
Gardenia
Geranium
Herbs
Honeysuckle (*Lonicera*)
Hydrangea
  (*Hydrangea paniculata*)
Icelandic poppy
  (*Papaver nudicaule*)
Kalanchoe
Lily
Marigold (*Calendula*)
Mind-your-own-business
  (*Helxine*)
Ox-eye daisy

Pelargonium
Peony
Philadelphus
Rose (garden varieties)
Rue (*Ruta*)
Sunflower
Tuberose
  (*Polianthes tuberosa*)
Wax-flower
  (*Stephanotis floribunda*)

Fall

Amaryllis
Bergenia leaves
Bouvardia
Crabapple
Cup-and-saucer vine
  (*Cobaea scandens*)
Echinops
Eucalyptus
Heather
Hydrangea
Icelandic poppy
  (*Papaver nudicaule*)
Ivy
Love-lies-bleeding
  (*Amaranthus caudatus*)
Nerine
Orchid
Snowberry
  (*Symphoricarpos albus*)
Stephanandra
Sunflower
Tuberose
  (*Polianthes tuberosa*)

Winter

African violet (*Saintpaulia*)
Amaryllis
Anemone

Calla (Arum) lily
  (*Zantedeschia aethiopica*)
Bergenia leaves
Box (*Buxus*)
Camellia foliage
Christmas rose
  (*Helleborus niger*)
Crocus
Cyclamen
Eucalyptus
Eucharis
Euphorbia fulgens
Fir
Garrya elliptica
Guelder rose
  (*Viburnum opulus*)
Holly
Hyacinth
Ivy
Jasmine
  (*Jasminum polyanthum*)
Lichen-covered branches
Narcissus 'Paper White'
Nerine
Orchid
Ruscus
Skimmia japonica
Snowdrop (*Galanthus nivalis*)
Tulip
Violet (*Viola odorata*)
Wax-flower
  (*Stephanotis floribunda*)
Winter cherry
  (*Solanum capsicastrum*)
Winter-flowering viburnums
Winter sweet
  (*Chimonanthus praecox*)
Witch hazel
  (*Hamamelis mollis*)
Yew (*Taxus baccata*)